ENERGY SHIFT

strategy+business

ENERGY SHIFT

Game-Changing Options for Fueling the Future

ERIC SPIEGEL
NEIL McARTHUR
WITH ROB NORTON

Mc
Graw
Hill

New York   Chicago   San Francisco   Lisbon   London
Madrid   Mexico City   Milan   New Delhi   San Juan
Seoul   Singapore   Sydney   Toronto

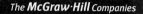
The *McGraw·Hill* Companies

Booz & Company is publisher of *strategy+business* magazine.

1 2 3 4 5 6 7 8 9 0 DOC/DOC 0 3 2 1 0 9

ISBN 978-0-07-150834-6
MHID   0-07-150834-1

Design by Lee Fukui and Mauna Eichner

McGraw-Hill books are available at special quantity discounts to use as premiums and sales promotions, or for use in corporate training programs. To contact a representative please visit the Contact Us pages at www.mhprofessional.com.

Special thanks to my wife Doreen, daughter Jessica, and son Allan for their understanding and support during the many nights and weekends that I worked on this book over the past year. Hopefully they will see the energy shift we describe in their lifetimes.

E.S.

For all my family, thank you for all your love, support, encouragement, and inspiration. Sylvia, thank you for your love and for opening new doors in my life. Annette, thank you for being a wonderful mother and friend. Kyle and Nicky, thank you for the joy you bring; may you grow up to be good global citizens in an environmentally conscious world.

N.M.

CONTENTS

LOOKING BEYOND UPHEAVAL

ENERGY PRICES are extraordinarily volatile, and have recently hit record highs. Economists worry about the effects on gross domestic product (GDP) growth. Politicians raise alarms about energy dependence and the security of foreign oil and gas supplies. Scientists warn of irreversible damage to the earth from the uncontrolled use of fossil fuels. There is much talk about conservation and alternative energy sources.

Welcome to . . . the late 1970s. For anyone who remembers that time, the crisis atmosphere surrounding energy since 2006 evokes more than a little déjà vu. It is tempting to take comfort in the fact that there was no economic apocalypse after the energy crises of the 1970s. Instead, most energy prices fell back to their earlier levels within a few years; governments, businesses, and consumers adapted; and the world economy not only survived but prospered. It's reasonable to wonder: why can't things go back to normal now, just as they did then?

But the similarities between the current energy situation and the 1970's oil crises are limited and somewhat superficial, and the differences are more pronounced. To be sure, many of the most critical factors are uncertain, particularly when the time it takes to change large-scale infrastructure is taken into account. But there's one thing we can say with confidence: the energy situation is not going back to normal, at least if "normal" means the industry structure and stability of the 1990s.

Every chief executive and senior manager today will be forced to confront the reality of uncertain and unstable energy markets over the next two decades or more. For leaders in organizations that are involved in energy production or that use energy as a key input, the impact will be immense. The structure of their industry will undergo significant change—slowly at first, but accelerating over time as early innovations succeed and the rest of the industry falls in step. All other businesses will be affected as well. The goods we produce, the devices we create, the computer systems we rely on, the transportation and logistics networks we use—all will depend on what happens to energy supply, demand, and prices.

This book will help you understand the major forces that are shaping the future of energy and the choices that will face leaders in all walks of life. It will help you distinguish the myths and misconceptions that you read in the newspaper from the actual situation and its implications for any business or organization, from the smallest local enterprise to the largest multinational.

The signs of discontinuity in the energy sector today are unmistakable. The most obvious is the spectacular volatility in energy prices, especially the price of petroleum, in the early twenty-first century. As recently as 2003, a barrel of crude oil sold for less than $30 in 2008 dollars—close to the inflation-adjusted level that it had trended around throughout the late 1980s and 1990s. Since then, however, the price has risen dramatically, to as high as $147 per barrel, far eclipsing its previous record high set during the oil shock that followed the Iranian Revolution in 1980 ($103.76 in 2008 dollars). A price of $100 per barrel, which seemed unthinkable a few years ago, became seen as unremarkable. Price increases for the other major fossil fuels—natural gas and coal—more than doubled over the same time period. The energy price runup was less sharp in Europe and other regions, since oil prices are denominated in dollars and the dollar had depreciated significantly relative to other currencies. Recent European oil prices went as high as €80, however, around the record set in the 1980s, adjusted for inflation. Then, during the financial crisis of autumn 2008, global oil prices suddenly fell to $50 a barrel—still a major net gain—leaving tremendous uncertainty about the future price.

In addition to the direct pain that energy costs inflict upon businesses and consumers, they are also pushing up the prices of many other goods. Rising energy costs, for instance, have contributed to a surge in world food prices. These have risen some 60 percent in the last few years and have produced deprivation (in some cases, provoking riots) in parts of the developing world. Prices of other commodities, including minerals and raw materials, have also risen rapidly. Such "second-order" factors, or other significant economic trends affected by changes in energy costs, are sending shocks through the economy. They present urgent problems for many managers who are struggling to maintain stable costs and revenues while engineering cleaner, greener operations for their companies.

Back in the 1970s, energy prices rose solely because of uncertainties about supply—specifically, about political instability in the Middle East. Today, the stability of the Middle East remains a concern, but more fundamental factors are driving this price rise. The current world energy situation is the result of three colliding long-term trends: the relentless increase in energy demand driven by world economic growth, the slow drop-off in crude oil and natural gas supplies from producers outside the Organization of Petroleum Exporting Countries (OPEC) and the former members of the Soviet Union (FSU), and an intensifying need to reduce greenhouse gas emissions. The result is a widening awareness that the way we have used energy in the past is unsustainable in the future.

The steep, sustained rise in worldwide energy demand slowed during the economic downturn of 2008 but will resume as growth returns. It is driven both by economic growth in the developed world and by the surging growth and rising populations of newly industrializing nations. Oil and natural gas production, meanwhile, has been leveling off since the late 1990s, and over the last five years, it has been consistently too slow to keep pace with demand. This new dynamic is a discontinuous, unprecedented change in the historical trend for energy supply and demand.

The other major difference between the last energy crisis and the current one is the level of concern about global warming. Environmentalists in the 1970s worried mostly about the effects of air pollution on health and the quality of life. Solving those problems seemed to be a matter of incremental change, achievable using existing technologies, and was not a matter of urgent public concern. Today, rising levels of greenhouse gas emissions have created widespread fear that energy use is endangering the earth's climate, and these emissions are a major focus of national and international policy debates. Public and political concerns about the urgency of the climate change problem continue to grow, convincing many former skeptics that comprehensive changes in energy policy and practice will be needed to forestall future damage.

For businesses, the concerns about climate change will have major implications. If the prices of high-carbon fossil fuels like petroleum and coal rise to reflect their environmental impact—which will happen if global climate-change regulation is enacted—then the basic business models of some industries, such as the power-generation industry, will change drastically. But all businesses will be significantly affected as higher prices spread across the world economy and lower-carbon alternatives become more competitive and more prevalent. What executives and decision makers need in this environment is a balanced and transparent understanding of their exposure to carbon-based fuels: the costs of these fuels, their advantages and drawbacks, and the alternatives that are available today or are under development. Exposure in the sense of dependence on a high-carbon fuel or one with uncertain supply could be as damaging as exposure in the sense of financial commitment to a risky investment. In the same way that well-managed investment firms limit their exposure to risk, well-managed energy consumers will start hedging and limiting their exposure to energy sources.

MYTHS AND REALITIES

If the energy realities are more daunting today than they were in the 1980s, the solutions are also very different. Last time, there was a pervasive move toward energy effi- ciency in some parts of the world (such as Japan) and ulti- mately a "return to normalcy" that took place naturally when OPEC's prices fell. A resolution of the current crisis will not happen by itself. It means finding a solution that ensures two seemingly incompatible things: first, that the world will have sufficient energy supplies to enable con- tinued economic growth in the developed world and con- tinued opportunity for newly industrializing nations, and second, that industrial society can slow or, better still, re- verse the increase in energy-related greenhouse gas emis- sions.

The only way this will happen is by accomplishing an *energy shift* that is unprecedented in history—a transition away from the carbon-intense fuels and technologies of the past. The shift has already started, as can be seen in everything from the rise of biofuels and hybrid autos to the building of large wind farms to the popular opposi- tion against the construction of new coal-burning power plants. But what we have seen so far is only the beginning of a vast reshaping of the energy landscape. The landscape as we know it took more than a century to develop, and it will take decades to shift to its new form. This transition will shape every aspect of business and daily life between now and 2030.

Life during an energy shift is rife with tension, and for good reason: the forces that are affecting this shift, and that will determine how quickly it can be accomplished, are still difficult to see clearly. A huge amount of information and analysis about the upheaval in the energy markets is churned out each month, but much of it reflects the biases of different industries, interest groups, and other constituencies. A good deal of this material is also imperfectly grounded in economic and business reality, and some of it is naïve.

One useful way to better understand your options is to start examining some of the persistent myths about energy, and the constituencies that benefit from their promulgation. These myths are relevant because they can drive public opinion, and hence public policy; and because business practices will also be based on these myths, in some cases leading to severe competitive disadvantage.

The Global Oil Depletion Myth

The world is running out of oil.

Reality

This myth has become popular among some environmentalists, antigrowth activists, and others promoting alternative energy sources and conservation and, in some cases, opposing industrialization and unfettered economic growth. It has also been popularized by an ongoing argument (often referred to as "peak oil"), based on some supply estimates, that the world has passed the maximum global petroleum production rate.

Belief in this myth is tempting, and it makes a compelling story. But it's not true. Despite the current imbalance between supply and demand in oil and other fossil fuels, and despite the peak oil view, the world is not running out of this substance. No matter what happens, long-term supplies will be available. There are plenty of fossil fuels still in the ground in existing reserves, and new reserves continue to be discovered in regions like Central Asia and South America. There are also vast proven reserves of "unconventional oil," which can be derived from oil sands, oil shale, and even coal. Using known technology, these sources could provide enough hydrocarbons to fuel a petroleum-based economy for many decades to come—if companies and policy makers are willing to deal with the environmental costs and higher prices. These sources could enhance energy security for many countries, including the United States, Brazil, Russia, China, and India.

However, in one sense, the depletion argument is right. The short- to medium-term constraints on oil supply are significant, especially those on cheap, easily recoverable oil. Unconventional oil sources are more expensive and are also likely to prove unacceptable from an environmental perspective unless expensive new technologies are deployed to limit greenhouse gas emissions. Therefore, while oil will remain abundant, it will not necessarily be the "easy oil" we have seen in the past, and oil will most likely play a much more limited role in the global economy post-2030.

The China Myth

Rising prices are all Asia's fault.

Reality

This myth has gained currency because it makes it easier for people in the West to ignore their own role in boosting energy prices. It places all the blame on the newly industrializing nations of Asia. It is true that the growth in energy demand in China—as well as in India and other industrializing nations—has been significant. And mainstream forecasts envision that energy demand in developing Asian countries will more than double over the next 30 years. A new middle class is rapidly acquiring cars, major appliances, and a more energy-intensive lifestyle, and its demands will echo those of consumers in the West.

But the full truth is more complicated. For one thing, price pressures can just as easily be blamed on growing energy demand in the *developed* world. Petroleum usage in North America, for instance, has increased as much as in China in the past 20 years. And underlying demand will continue to grow in the United States and other mature economies.

Also, demand is only part of the price equation. One reason that prices remained low during the 1980s and 1990s was that oil production from nations outside OPEC and the former Soviet Union was growing steadily. This reflected the development of new reserves in the North Sea, Canada, Mexico, and Brazil, among other places. Non-OPEC and non-FSU production, however, began to flatten in the late 1990s and actually declined starting after 2002, as output and reserves in established oil-producing nations like the United States dwindled and fewer new reserves were found. Since then, the OPEC producers who control the most economic and easily recoverable oil and gas reserves in the Middle East have been straining to increase their capacity to produce more oil, but they have not been able (or willing) to do so quickly enough to keep pace with demand. More broadly, the supply crunch has extended across the energy spectrum. The costs of supplying other forms of energy have also climbed in recent years as a result of a dramatic rise in the costs of production equipment such as coal-mining machinery, liquid natural gas (LNG) terminals, refinery vessels, and infrastructure of all kinds.

The "Easy Ethanol" Myth

Biofuels are the green solution for transportation.

Reality

This myth is promoted by those in the agricultural sector who stand to benefit from the development of biofuels, and by those in countries like the United States and Brazil whose first priority is energy security. It is also a seemingly attractive story for environmentalists. And there are some reasons to be optimistic about the biofuel potential. Ethanol made from sugarcane, in particular, is a viable alternative today to petroleum; biofuels made from other sources such as cellulose, algae, and waste products could contribute a significant volume to the fuel pool, especially if the supply of agricultural land expands.

But from an environmental perspective, the biofuels available today are estimated to save from 20 percent (corn ethanol) to 80 percent or higher (sugarcane and cellulosic ethanol) in greenhouse gas emissions. This is at best neutral, and in some cases harmful, once the effects of land use are factored in: the impact on climate change of continuing to farm land that would otherwise revert to grassland or forest. Biofuels have also been implicated in food shortages and rising food prices. Since food and petroleum prices are inevitably linked, the impact of biofuels on gasoline prices may be muted. And there are water scarcity issues as well; countries that face water shortages may simply not be able to expand into biofuel production.

Even the next generation of cellulosic biofuels may not solve these problems in the short run. In the long run, with enough technological development, some futuristic biofuel approaches, like algae-derived biofuels that don't require large amounts of land, could someday prove to be a long-term alternative to petroleum. But these will take decades to come to fruition, with many obstacles along the way.

The Carbon-Free Power Myth

We can meet the world's needs for electric power and reduce greenhouse gas emissions within a decade or two relatively painlessly by switching to carbon-free renewable energy sources such as solar, wind, and geothermal energy.

Reality

This myth resonates deeply with those who are concerned about the environment, because it tells people what they most want to hear. And it's true that these renewable energy sources—especially wind and solar power—hold tremendous promise for the future, and ultimately may hold much of the answer to global climate change (and to many countries' concerns about energy security). But today they supply only a few percent of electric power generation, and significant technological breakthroughs in storage and efficiency, as well as massive investments in transmission infrastructure, will need to be made before renewables can compete on a wide scale, cost-effectively, with traditional fuels. Even using optimistic assumptions about renewables, much of the world's electric power needs in 2030 will be filled, as they are today, by fossil fuels. However, the next 20 years are likely to see renewables taking larger percentage shares in power generation, and will lay the groundwork for a more significant shift to lower-carbon and carbon-free sources in the future.

The No-Nukes Myth

Nuclear energy is dead.

Reality

This myth plays on the safety fears that grew out of past nuclear power accidents. It still has currency among some environmentalists (although others are now less opposed, as a result of their awareness of global climate change). As a result, much of the debate about meeting future energy needs tends to ignore the positive potential for more nuclear capacity.

Today, nuclear energy from 439 reactors supplies some 15 percent of power-generation needs around the world. In some nations, it commands a very large market share.

France derives more than 80 percent of its electricity from nuclear energy; Japan's nuclear share is 35 percent; in the United States, it is 20 percent. Moreover, despite persistent fears about safety, the nuclear industry has an excellent record, with the exception of the Chernobyl disaster of 1986. Concerns remain about the proliferation and storage of nuclear waste, about the availability of uranium for nuclear fuel, and about the potential link between nuclear energy production and nuclear weapons production, but these issues, while significant, may not in themselves slow down the advance of this technology.

The main advantages of nuclear energy are that it is a dependable, around-the-clock power supply, and that it produces no greenhouse gases, making it the most scalable current power-generation technology that does not contribute to global warming. Currently, there are plans to build more than 200 new nuclear plants worldwide, although rising costs and supply-chain problems are slowing the industry's growth. In light of concerns about global warming, nuclear energy will remain an essential part of the electric power mix in the future.

The Private-Sector Solution Myth

Industry alone can bring about the energy shift.

Reality
This myth is the result of the mistrust concerning the ability of government to play a positive role in resolving long-term economic problems that have grown up in some major countries, including the United States. It is promulgated by supporters of a limited role for the public sector. But

while it is true that private entrepreneurs and corporations accomplish most of the world's innovation and operate many of its energy businesses, it is also true that historically, major shifts in energy markets have been driven by governments executing long-term strategies. Developments like France's embrace of nuclear power, Brazil's creation of a sugarcane-based ethanol industry, the rise of wind power in Denmark (and now in the United States), and the development of solar power in Germany were all rooted in government policy choices. Given the magnitude of the challenge that the energy shift presents, it's clear that government decisions, public-private initiatives, and tax incentives will be necessary components in achieving major technological breakthroughs and building new energy infrastructure. The current electric power grid and transportation systems could not have been constructed without heavy government involvement; the same is true of the emerging infrastructure that will replace them.

CONTRADICTIONS AND EXPECTATIONS

In short, the realities of energy in this century are contradicting perceptions—and expectations—from all quarters. On the one hand, the economics of fossil fuels are moving to a new equilibrium. Current energy supplies are proving inadequate in the short run to meet rising energy demand, and prices are rising in response.

At the same time, the scientific consensus on the dangers of global warming has coalesced. This conviction cannot be ignored or dismissed: civilization needs to sharply slow the growth of greenhouse gases to avoid irreparable damage to the environment. This will limit companies' and nations' options for meeting future energy needs. And it will accelerate the shift away from fossil fuels to more sustainable forms of energy.

Even as recently as 2005, this conclusion could not have been stated with the same authoritativeness. Scientists and environmentalists have been warning of the dangers of greenhouse gas emissions (notably carbon dioxide, or CO_2) for nearly 30 years. But many people had considered the scientific evidence to be inconclusive. Public concern in the United States and some other countries was muted, and important constituencies—including the U.S. government and segments of the global business community—had been hesitant to support policy action to mitigate global warming.

The paradigm, however, has shifted sharply in the past few years. Today, the debate about global climate change is effectively over. There is widespread recognition that the dangers of global warming are real and that our use of fossil fuels is the chief source of destabilizing greenhouse gas emissions. In that context, of course, debates will continue: about how to clean up CO_2 emissions, how to pay for that cleanup (especially in the developing world), and how to cope with the effects of climate change.

Concerns about the security of energy supplies will also constrain future energy choices. Energy security has become an increasingly important consideration in national policies, for both national security and geopolitical reasons. In the United States, dependence on oil from OPEC is driving energy security concerns; in Europe, concerns revolve around dependence on imported natural gas supplies, particularly from Russia. In Asia, concerns about securing sufficient supplies for continued industrialization and GDP growth are paramount. Many countries, including China and the United States, are actively moving to secure future energy supplies to prepare for a possibly more resource- and carbon-constrained future.

And finally, the expectations of the public require more energy than ever before. Even the world's low-income people are acquiring and using cell phones and electric lights; the wealthiest are traveling more than ever; and vast, energy-using server farms are meeting the world's intense new demand for information services. Nor are prevailing energy habits likely to change. For more than 100 years, petroleum, natural gas, and coal have been cheap and plentiful. This has given rise to the colossal industries that dominated the corporate landscape of the twentieth century, from the energy industry itself to steel, railroads, automobile manufacturers, airlines, home appliances, and modern manufacturing. It also required the construction of the vast energy infrastructure of wells, mines, refineries, transport systems, pipelines, electric grids, and retail outlets that girdles the earth today. If people take all this for granted, they can hardly be blamed for doing so. Somehow or other, a lifestyle based on energy abundance will be maintained.

THE PACE OF CHANGE

On some level, the shift is already under way. The recent price surge has made traditional fuels more expensive and is creating market conditions in which alternative energy sources (both renewable fuels such as ethanol, biodiesel, wind, and solar and "unconventional" oil and natural gas) can compete with conventional fossil fuels if prices remain anywhere near recent levels. In the past, the expense of these alternatives discouraged research, development, and commercialization; in many cases, promising projects launched after the last oil shock were abandoned in the 1980s when oil prices fell. Efforts to encourage energy conservation undertaken back then were relaxed or abandoned in many countries for the same reasons. Now, with higher energy prices in place for at least half a decade, innovation and the rollout of new technologies will accelerate. The result will, in the end, be a wholesale change in the infrastructure underlying human civilization.

But even so, results will appear on a much slower timeline than many consumers and citizens expect, and probably much too slowly to offset the rise in global temperatures that alarms climate scientists. The reason is not primarily a gap in research and technology. One delaying factor is the inherent amount of time it takes to move from one technology to another at a global scale. Another delaying factor is the built-in resistance grounded in the installed base of power and transportation systems around the world.

The oil and gas, automobile, and electric power industries are among the world's biggest and most capital-intensive. Companies have made massive investments in production facilities and infrastructure over many decades, and thus many of them have strong incentives to preserve the status quo. Even where companies are eager to adapt and change, or where new companies, backed by venture

capital, enter the market, the lags between the introduc-
tion of new fuels and technologies and their wide availability are long. It takes years to design and build new
models of cars, to construct the infrastructure for biofuels
or windfarms, or to build nuclear power plants. Worse
still, the sharp rise in demand for new energy plants and
infrastructure of all kinds is outstripping the supply of
available equipment and trained personnel and is straining supply chains across the sector. Many executives are
understandably hesitant to make large "bet the company"
investments until they know more about the environmental and tax structures in which they will have to operate in
the future. Major companies are devising strategies for
survival in whatever environment prevails.

It will thus be difficult to see major changes in the
world's use of energy sources over the next decade, and
perhaps for much longer. As a result, fossil fuels will continue to supply most of the world's energy needs, and the
challenge for government and industry will be to find ways
to meet future demand while developing technologies and
strategies that will mitigate the production of greenhouse
gases. The burden of meeting this challenge will fall most
heavily on the electricity generation industry, which in
most countries is heavily dependent on coal—the fuel that
will be producing the greatest amount of greenhouse gases
in the future. Companies that rely heavily on energy as a
primary input (steelmakers, aluminum smelters, and concrete manufacturers) will also be challenged, as will automakers and their extensive chains of suppliers.

These realities help explain the common projections,
like those made by the United States Energy Department

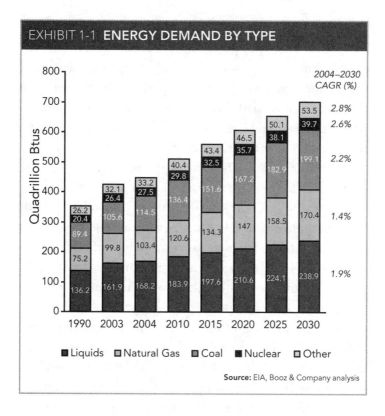

EXHIBIT 1-1 ENERGY DEMAND BY TYPE

2004–2030 CAGR (%)

Source: EIA, Booz & Company analysis

in 2007 (see Exhibit 1-1), which show rising total demand with all energy sources growing to meet it in somewhat the same proportions that they have today. The energy shift may be slow enough to look like this in 2030. Or it may be accelerated. A decision maker in the late 2000s would be wise to be prepared for either eventuality.

The energy shift will play out most visibly in the two biggest energy-using sectors: transportation and electric power production. After a century of reliance on petroleum-fueled vehicles and coal-fired generating plants, both will be transformed over the next few decades. In the meantime, corporate leaders in these sectors will face a series of challenges. How can they position their businesses in the face of this uncertainty? What form of energy shift will best serve them, and how can they contribute to making sure that this form is viable? And if the energy shift is coming, how rapidly should they adapt—or shift their own operations and take a leadership role?

This last question is perhaps the most critical. It may be possible to speed up the energy shift in some ways, and some sectors—for example, the automobile industry, with its forays into electric, hydrogen, compressed natural gas (CNG), and hybrid vehicles—are already confounding the expectations of a year ago. But even the most activist, optimistic initiatives operate within powerful constraints. The installed base of capital equipment represents a powerful delaying factor, as does the uneven and uncertain pace of technological development. The most significant source of delay, however, is the different time frames needed for investment in various components of the energy system, from exploration and production of fuel sources to their distribution to the manufacture of consumer goods like automobiles.

Companies and countries that "bet conservative"—that don't invest in new technologies and assume that the old technologies will dominate—are likely to win in the short run, but they may well find themselves unprepared as the shift unfolds. Meanwhile, companies and countries that "bet bold"—that assume that the new technologies will supersede—will encounter many challenges and difficulties at first. However, some of them will be the leaders of the global economy in the long run. And in order to play that leading role, they have to start now.

In other words, there is an impasse (partly technological, partly embedded in the business environment) that
is both defining and constraining the energy shift. In order
to break that impasse, some kind of concerted action may
be needed—perhaps by industry, probably by government.
It is possible that energy prices, if they remain near their
recent record levels or rise even further, may prove powerful enough to break the impasse. But it is not enough to
count on high prices as a substitute for policy change. That
is too short-term and too shortsighted. Oil prices will go up
and down. As was seen in the 2008 U.S. presidential campaign, proposals based on price relief often have a glib
or short-term focus, such as gas-tax holidays or expansion of offshore drilling. If decisions rest solely on oil
costs, the world may simply continue as it is, "muddling
through" as the impasse gradually erodes, and will have to
cope with shortages, price oscillations, and climate change
along the way.

DEMAND AND SUPPLY

This book is not an encyclopedia about the future of energy, nor does it delve deeply into the specifics of each potential new fuel and technological advance. Many of these,
from solar energy and tidal power to advanced biofuels,
may become important in future decades, but they are not
likely to have a major effect any time soon. Instead, this
book is a compact guide to the major trends that are driving the energy shift today and that are likely to have the
greatest impact over the next two decades.

The story starts with an analysis of the continued
strong demand for energy of all kinds in the developed

world and the vast new demand coming from the newly industrializing nations. We then examine the slowdown in production from conventional oil supplies and its implications for the future of transportation. While this includes the emerging alternatives of biofuels, electricity, and hydrogen, we also examine less trendy subjects, such as the fact that only half the petroleum consumed today is used in transportation—which means that the potential supplies for transportation may be much larger than is commonly believed. Next comes an analysis of the fossil fuels (coal and natural gas) that currently supply most electricity generation, the ways the mix will change as the world increasingly moves to lower-carbon and carbon-free fuels, like nuclear, solar, and wind, and the challenges this will present for the power generation industry.

The concluding chapter looks at the major areas of uncertainty that make it difficult to see how—and especially, how fast—the energy shift is likely to unfold over the next 20 years. In each of these areas—greenhouse gas regulation, energy security, and the pace of technological change—we examine specific trends, developments, and events that will serve as leading indicators for assessing how fast the energy shift is proceeding. In greenhouse gas regulation, for example, much attention is currently focused on how the United States will change during the Obama administration; a more crucial question is whether the leading developed nations will be able to reach an enforceable accord with the leading industrializing nations. In energy security, most analyses look narrowly at petroleum; the security of natural gas supplies may be just as important. In automotive technology, the conventional wisdom says that a single new approach to energy for transportation will emerge to dominate the market. More likely, there will be diverse and competing approaches. The most important single indicator of where the market is going in the near future will be the pace of improvement in battery capacity.

Amidst all the uncertainty about the future of energy, however, one thing is certain: the energy shift is already happening, and it will continue. And as it proceeds, it will rearrange—and transform—the commercial, industrial, and consumer landscapes of the world throughout the twenty-first century. For business leaders, the status quo is not an option. The corporate energy policies that have been adequate in the past will be inadequate for dealing with the changes set in motion by the energy shift. The energy choices that many companies make today will help determine their future competitive advantage. But the energy shift is complex, and investments cannot be made lightly. Your optimal choices will depend on the industry you're in, the role you want to play, and the demands of your market. The best options will often involve significant internal change for many large energy and transportation companies. It's still not clear how many of them will be up to the challenge.

THE RELENTLESS DEMAND FOR ENERGY

THE GREATEST SINGLE FACTOR in setting the stage for an energy shift is the demand for electricity and transportation fuel around the world. Rising demand for energy is a fact of life for the modern consumer economy. World usage of energy of all types has been increasing at an average annual rate of 2.6 percent per year since the 1960s. As noted in Chapter 1, because of the increase in sources of supply, this rise in demand was not reflected in the oil price for years. But in the early 2000s, the price finally caught up.

The price may well fluctuate from month to month, especially as the financial meltdown of 2008 plays itself out and the global recession unfolds. But no matter how prices change in the short term, the relentless growth in energy use will continue over the long term. Slower growth in the developed world will be offset by faster growth in developing nations. By 2030, according to standard projections of population and economic growth from the U.S. government's Energy Information Association (EIA), world energy demand will have undergone a net increase of 57 percent from a 2004 base, with most of the increases in the fossil fuels—petroleum, coal, and natural gas—that currently supply the vast bulk of the world's needs. These and other projections, which use mainstream economic forecasts of economic growth and assume no major changes in existing law or policy, provide a starting point for analyzing future energy trends.

To fill this demand, a mix of fuels will be needed; and as we saw in Chapter 1, demand for just about every source of energy in use today is expected to increase. In the EIA forecast, this mix of fuel sources is not expected to change very dramatically over the next two decades. This is partly because the forecast assumes no changes in current government policy, and also because it assumes that crude oil prices will fall back from their recent highs to $49 per barrel, adjusted for inflation, by 2014, and then increase only to $59 per barrel by 2030. Some private-sector analysts have predicted higher price levels; if they're correct, or if government policies do shift, then the mix could conceivably change.

But even if there are changes, the current proportion of energy sources will play an enormous role in determining the energy mix of the future. More than 86 percent of world energy demand today is met by fossil fuels. Liquid fuels (primarily petroleum products) account for almost half of that; they made up 36 percent of world energy use in 2007. Demand for these fuels is driven powerfully by continuing

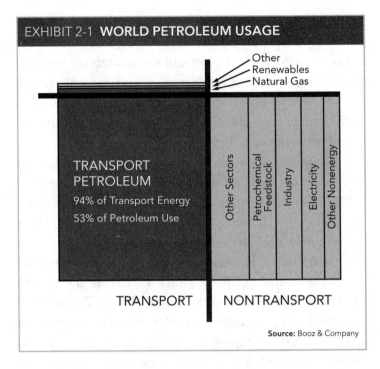

EXHIBIT 2-1 WORLD PETROLEUM USAGE

Other
Renewables
Natural Gas

TRANSPORT
PETROLEUM

94% of Transport Energy

53% of Petroleum Use

Other Sectors

Petrochemical Feedstock

Industry

Electricity

Other Nonenergy

TRANSPORT · NONTRANSPORT

Source: Booz & Company

reliance on gasoline and diesel oil for transportation. Petroleum provides 94 percent of world transport energy. But that is only part of the story. As Exhibit 2-1 shows, nearly half of the petroleum produced is currently used for nontransportation needs—for power generation, in industrial processes, or as feedstocks for petrochemical manufacturing. Demand for nontransport petroleum has been weakening in recent years, but not nearly enough to offset the increase in demand for transportation fuels.

Nonpetroleum alternatives to transportation fuels, shown in the diagram above the black line, are also part of the mix; these include biofuels (mostly ethanol and biodiesel), plus natural gas (used in some vehicles), and even some electricity. As we'll see in Chapter 4, these may be a

27

major long-term component of the energy shift. But they currently supply only a tiny fraction of world demand for transportation fuels. Significant technological advances, major infrastructure investments, and possible policy changes will be necessary before they will be produced in sufficient quantities to fill a significant fraction of the demand for petroleum-based fuels.

The demand for coal, which supplied 29 percent of world energy demand in 2007 (up from 26 percent in 2004), parallels the demand for electricity. For a century, coal has generated most of the base load electricity (the minimum level of power that must be supplied to meet the expected level of customer demand throughout the year) for many of the world's regions, including the United States and major parts of Europe and Asia. Demand for coal has been particularly strong over the last few years as demand from developing nations like China and India has increased. The EIA's projections show the demand for coal increasing faster than the demand for any other fuel except renewables, to 28 percent of total energy demand by 2030, as coal plays an increasingly larger role in electricity production.

As we will see in Chapter 5, coal has significant pluses and minuses. On the plus side, coal is the most abundant fossil fuel in the world, and much of it is located in energy-hungry nations, including China, India, Russia, and North America. The United States, for example, is sometimes called "the Saudi Arabia of coal," since its reserves are the world's largest. But on the downside, coal produces more greenhouse gases per unit of energy than any other energy source, and environmentalists have increasingly opposed expanded—or even continued—coal use. "Clean coal" technologies that could eliminate greenhouse gas emissions during coal combustion exist, but they have not yet been deployed on a commercial scale and would increase the cost significantly.

Natural gas accounted for 24 percent of world energy use in 2007, and demand is driven by its use in home heating, industrial processes and, increasingly, electric power generation. In the 1990s, natural gas was favored for producing electricity because it was less expensive than alternatives such as oil and coal. Although price increases have reduced its competitiveness, it is still seen as an attractive fuel source because of both its efficiency and its relatively low production of greenhouse gases. Demand for natural gas has been increasing steadily since the 1970s, but has accelerated in recent years. In the United States, for example, demand from the electric power industry increased 10 percent in 2007.

In the past, natural gas was mostly produced and consumed in local or regional markets, since the most efficient way to transport it is by pipeline. In recent years, however, the rise of the technology and infrastructure for liquefying natural gas and transporting it in tankers has created an international market. As we'll see in Chapter 6, large amounts of natural gas have been discovered in the United States in unconventional sources such as shale; in addition, huge reserves of coal-bed methane may be tapped in countries with plentiful coal reserves. The net effect is threefold: first, natural gas prices still vary (as much as 30 percent between some regions). Second, for the moment, they are increasingly behaving as though they are linked to the world oil price. Third, they may drop and unhinge from oil prices as the supply of natural gas expands.

Renewables such as wind energy, solar power, and hydroelectric power account for 7 percent of the total, and are mostly provided by hydroelectric power. Nuclear energy provides 6 percent. Demand for these energy sources is also going to increase, but for the foreseeable future it will be limited, as we shall see, by the industry's ability to provide it at competitive costs.

THE DYNAMICS OF GLOBAL DEMAND

The dynamics of energy demand vary between developed and developing countries. In developing economies, per capita energy use rises steadily with income as people move out of poverty and can afford to live in larger homes, purchase more appliances, and own motor vehicles. In mature, industrialized economies, energy use per capita is already at a comparatively high level. Demand increases as incomes rise, but not as much as it would increase in developing nations, since much of the money spent on energy-consuming goods (such as appliances) simply replaces older goods with new ones (that are often more energy-efficient). Similarly, per capita petroleum use changes very little as incomes grow in the advanced industrial economies of Europe. Overall, economies become generally less "energy intense" as they grow and mature, using less energy per unit of GDP.

But the relatively slow demand growth in the industrial nations that make up the OECD (Organisation for Economic Co-operation and Development)—with an average growth rate of 0.8 percent per year—is offset by faster growth rates in developing countries. As seen in Exhibit 2-2, growth in

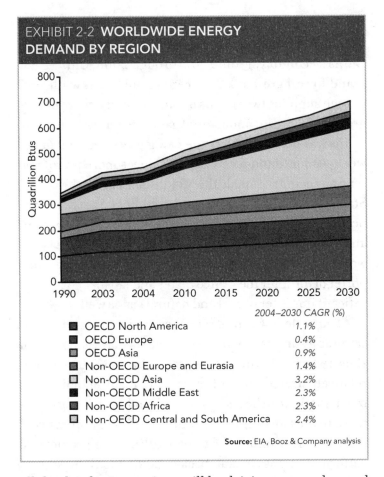

EXHIBIT 2-2 **WORLDWIDE ENERGY DEMAND BY REGION**

	2004–2030 CAGR (%)
■ OECD North America	1.1%
■ OECD Europe	0.4%
◻ OECD Asia	0.9%
■ Non-OECD Europe and Eurasia	1.4%
◻ Non-OECD Asia	3.2%
■ Non-OECD Middle East	2.3%
■ Non-OECD Africa	2.3%
◻ Non-OECD Central and South America	2.4%

Source: EIA, Booz & Company analysis

all the developing regions will be driving energy demand in the future. Energy consumption in these nations is expected to grow at an annual rate of 2.6 percent, with the fastest rate, 3.2 percent, coming in non-OECD Asia, which is dominated by China and India. The overall increase in non-OECD Asia will be 128 percent. To put this in context, it means that just the increase in demand in non-OECD Asia will amount to more than the total current energy demand in North America.

The single greatest factor pushing up this demand is, of course, the spectacular growth and industrialization of China's economy. From 2001 through 2006, China's demand for oil grew at a 9 percent annual rate, while coal (which supplies two-thirds of China's total energy needs) grew at 12 percent and natural gas at 16 percent. In 2008, China was building about one new gigawatt coal plant per week. As for liquid fuel, China produces more petroleum than any country outside the Middle East except the United States, Russia, and Mexico, and until 1993 it was a net exporter. Imports have risen steadily since then, however, and have accounted for a third of the total increase in world oil consumption. China is now the third largest importer of oil, after the United States and Japan, and is a significant importer of coal and natural gas as well.

The scale of China's recent surge in energy demand came as a surprise to most economists and analysts, and shows why predicting future growth in energy demand—a relatively straightforward exercise for mature, industrialized nations—can be tricky for newly industrializing countries. In the late twentieth century, the energy intensity of the Chinese economy had been falling in a predictable pattern. Partly as a result, back in 2000, the Chinese government and Western energy analysts were predicting that energy demand in China would grow 3 to 4 percent per year through 2010. In fact, energy demand grew at two to three times that rate. What the forecasters missed was the unprecedented growth in China's industrial sector, especially in energy-intensive basic manufacturing. China now accounts for almost half of world production of cement and flat glass, more than a third of global steel production, and over a quarter of global aluminum production. To fuel this manufacturing activity, China's energy intensity increased. By 2006, industry in China accounted for 72 percent of final energy consumption, compared to 31 percent in Europe and 25 percent in the United States. As the manufacturing sector fuels further economic growth, overall energy demand will continue to rise, although manufacturing's share will decline.

But to blame China for the current energy crisis is to single out only one of the actors in a larger historical drama. Overall global energy demand rises with both population and GDP. World population is expected to grow from 6.6 billion in 2007 to 8.4 billion in 2030. Overall world GDP growth, adjusted for inflation, is projected to be 4.1 percent per year. Industrialized nations—the members of OECD—will grow at a 2.5 percent annual rate; growth in the developing nations will be 5.3 percent. In short, while China's growth is immense, it will not be alone.

SLOWING DEMAND GROWTH

To slow the growth of this wave of energy demand would require unprecedented attention to energy conservation. The potential gains from this sort of conservation are large. Merely switching from traditional incandescent lightbulbs to energy-efficient fluorescent models, for example, could save 70 percent of the electricity used for lighting. The long list of obvious improvements includes better insulation for buildings, better maintenance of heating systems to reduce leakage, "smart" thermostats that turn down automatically at night, more energy-efficient appliances, and more efficient power-generation equipment and transmission lines.

But history shows that despite exhortations from environmentalists, consumers are unlikely to practice conservation when the financial gains are small and the societal gains are diffuse. There are only two factors that might conceivably lead to greater levels of conservation, or at least that have done so in the past. The first is government policy, for example, seeking to forestall the dangers of global climate change. Big gains from energy conservation tend to come when there is concerted policy action (reflecting political leadership and widespread support from citizens). Unfortunately, this has proved effective in only a few countries in the past.

The second is if energy prices rise high enough to change peoples' behavior, as happened after the energy crises and resulting price increases in the 1970s. The future course of energy demand—and the future of global warming—will thus depend in large part on the future path of energy prices.

Energy demand is generally slow to react to price increases in the short term. Consumers often have few alternatives when fuel prices rise. For an automobile owner with a typical gasoline-powered car, for instance, the only short-term response to rising prices is to pay more or drive less, perhaps by carpooling to work or cutting back on recreational driving. While people can opt to buy smaller, more fuel-efficient cars, the effect on demand will be slow until the changeover is widespread enough to affect the overall composition of the national auto fleet.

Over the long term, energy demand does indeed respond powerfully to price changes, as consumers change their buying and usage patterns and manufacturers change their product mixes. This takes time, however. Capital must be reallocated, plant and equipment must be changed, and commercial and industrial users must shift to whichever energy source is most cost-advantageous.

In the United States, demand began to react to the cumulative price increase in 2007, as motorists cut back the number of miles driven for the first time in 20 years. Public use of mass transportation rose to its highest level in 50 years, and auto buyers indeed began favoring smaller, more fuel-efficient models. Sales of full-sized sport-utility vehicles and pickup trucks fell by double-digit percentages, while sales of small cars and hybrids boomed. In Europe, diesel-powered vehicles, which are more fuel-efficient and produce fewer greenhouse gas emissions, continue to increase their market share—now more than 50 percent of all new auto sales.

If energy prices hold at or near their recent high levels or rise further, future demand growth may be significantly lower than the standard forecasts have been anticipating, and the energy shift may happen more quickly, resulting in more noticeable changes in the mix of fossil and non-fossil fuels by 2030. If, however, energy prices fall back significantly in the future, in the same way that prices receded in the 1980s after the first oil shock, change will come more slowly, if it comes at all.

3

OIL'S PRODUCTION
PLATEAU

ONE OF THE PERSISTENT myths about energy, one that has been repeated for decades, is that the world is about to run out of oil. In its most extreme form, this myth, promulgated in films and popular books, prophesies that the rapid depletion of petroleum resources will shortly lead to a worldwide depression, mass starvation, and the end of civilization as we know it.

The good news is that it's not true. There is still plenty of "conventional" petroleum in the world, with more being discovered each year, and there are also vast potential supplies of "unconventional" oil that can be produced from known reserves of oil sands, oil shale, natural gas, and coal. But the bad news is that oil *production* has not kept up with increasing demand over the last several years. This is largely because output stopped rising and started falling in many oil-producing nations. The nations where output continues at the same or expanded levels are mainly members of OPEC or the former Soviet Union nations. These nations tend to be less interested in boosting supply unless it serves their own political interests.

This supply-demand imbalance is the primary reason for the record run-up in energy prices in the 2000s, and it is unlikely to turn around substantially any time soon. Current production sources can supply the roughly 85 million barrels per day that the world uses now, and will be able to do so for many years. These sources can probably supply an additional several million barrels per day, but they seem likely to flatten out at that level, even as demand is expected to continue rising. While this certainly doesn't mean the end of the world as we know it, it does mean that oil will continue to be more expensive in the future than it was in the not-so-distant past. It also means that in the medium term, the world will be increasingly dependent on OPEC in general and Saudi Arabia in particular for oil supplies. That, in turn, suggests a continuation of high and volatile prices and of concerns in some oil-importing countries about the security of energy supplies.

How high will oil prices go? As the price per barrel rose to $147 in mid-2008, some Wall Street analysts were predicting that oil could rise as high as $200 over the next several years. In June 2008, Russia's Gazprom predicted that oil prices would hit $250 in 2009. Most industry analysts, however, predicted that the long-term price of oil would be considerably lower than that. They were vindicated after the financial crisis of October 2008, when the price of oil fell back below $70. But that was still a significant net leap above the conventional oil industry assumption of just a few years before, when most analysts believed the price would not go above $25 per barrel.

One can never predict oil prices with certainty; but it is reasonable to expect that the price from 2009 through 2012 or 2015 will continue to stay well above its level of the low-cost 1990s. Over the longer term, continued growth in demand and relatively high prices may encourage the discovery and development of additional conventional sources of oil, but unlike the relatively cheap, easily recoverable oil that was available in the past, the oil of tomorrow will be found in more remote places, and in oil fields where drilling is more difficult and expensive. High prices will also increase the relative attractiveness of unconventional oil sources that were not cost-effective in the past. Energy companies are already producing more than 1 million barrels per day from oil sands in Canada. (These tarlike mineral deposits contain heavy forms of oil that cost more than conventional oil to recover and refine, and are discussed later in this chapter.) Canadian producers are planning to increase production, and if prices continue to rise, producing oil from even more expensive unconventional sources, such as oil shale, natural gas, and coal, will become cost-effective as well. Exploiting these unconventional sources, however, could significantly increase greenhouse gas emissions. And the current production of 1 million barrels per day is just 1.2 percent of current consumption, so production from unconventional sources would have to grow exponentially to take a large market share from conventional oil.

Rising demand and high prices will also make other alternative fuels more attractive. Biofuels, such as ethanol and biodiesel, are already competitive with petroleum at recent prices, and nonliquid alternative transportation fuels, such as electricity and hydrogen, could eventually be far less expensive. But neither of these alternatives is likely to displace petroleum to a significant degree in the next two decades. As detailed in the next chapter, concerns about the environmental impact of the current generation of biofuels, plus technological obstacles to the commercialization of new and improved varieties, will slow the market penetration of biofuels for at least a decade. And while hybrid cars (which combine electric batteries with internal combustion engines to improve fuel efficiency) are already popular and may gain market share, technological breakthroughs are needed before cars that run on pure electricity or hydrogen can be produced on a mass scale.

In the long run, higher oil prices will affect the growth of demand for oil. This will happen first with the demand for oil for nontransportation uses, such as for petrochemical feedstocks, industrial processes, and electricity generation. Nontransportation petroleum use has been declining since the first oil shocks of the 1970s but still accounts for nearly half of world oil used. High prices will continue to shift these users to other fuels, especially natural gas. High prices will also encourage the shift to other sources of energy for transportation, such as biofuels, electricity, and hydrogen.

THE NON-OPEC SLOWDOWN

The idea that the world is about to run out of oil is grounded in the "peak oil" theory, which suggests, quite reasonably, that at some point the world will reach a maximum level of global oil production, after which oil reserves will be consistently and inevitably exhausted. This theory, first for-

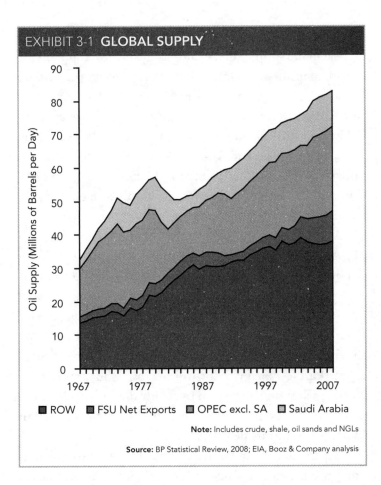

EXHIBIT 3-1 GLOBAL SUPPLY

Oil Supply (Millions of Barrels per Day)

■ ROW ■ FSU Net Exports ■ OPEC excl. SA ■ Saudi Arabia

Note: Includes crude, shale, oil sands and NGLs

Source: BP Statistical Review, 2008; EIA, Booz & Company analysis

mulated in the 1950s, has correctly predicted the peak oil moment for specific countries, such as the United States, where oil production peaked in the late 1960s, but predictions made in the 1970s that the world peak would occur in the 1990s turned out to be incorrect. One reason was that the oil shocks and price increases of the 1970s caused major reactions around the world. As noted in the last chapter, the growth rate of demand for petroleum slowed, as some nations adopted conservation policies and consumers in many markets shifted to more fuel-efficient autos. On the supply side, exploration and development for new oil supplies accelerated, and oil production outside OPEC kept increasing. (See Exhibit 3-1.) The increasing non-OPEC production came both from the FSU countries, led by Russia, and from new discoveries in places like the North Sea, Alaska, and Western Africa. These new sources boosted world production from the mid-1980s through the mid-1990s, and helped keep supply and demand in rough balance.

As the exhibit shows, however, supplies from the "rest of the world" flattened in the mid-1990s and have been declining more recently, as have supplies from the FSU nations. This reflects the depletion of reserves in many non-OPEC regions. The output from Alaska's largest field, Prudhoe Bay, for example, has fallen by more than two-thirds from its peak in the 1980s. Norway's production is more than a quarter below its peak in 2001, and other North Sea oil fields are also in steady decline. In Mexico, production at Pemex, the state-owned oil firm, has fallen 15 percent since its peak in 2004.

Worldwide, fewer giant oil fields have been discovered and brought online since 2000 than in any decade since the early twentieth century. Consequently, additions to world reserves have fallen to near their all-time lows. (See Exhibit 3-2.)

Most of the additions to worldwide reserves anticipated over the next several years are expected to be in the Middle East. The net effect has been to reduce the amount of spare production capacity (which determines the markets' ability to smooth out short-term imbalances of supply and demand) to historically low levels, and almost all

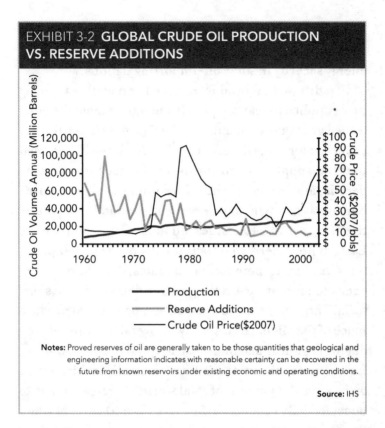

EXHIBIT 3-2 **GLOBAL CRUDE OIL PRODUCTION VS. RESERVE ADDITIONS**

— Production

— Reserve Additions

— Crude Oil Price($2007)

Notes: Proved reserves of oil are generally taken to be those quantities that geological and engineering information indicates with reasonable certainty can be recovered in the future from known reservoirs under existing economic and operating conditions.

Source: IHS

of that capacity over the next several years will be provided by Saudi Arabia.

As a result, it seems likely that oil-importing nations will become increasingly dependent on OPEC to meet future demand. In 2005, OPEC accounted for 42 percent of world oil production; by 2030, as non-OPEC reserve growth slows, forecasts by the International Energy Agency (IEA) show that OPEC will be called upon to supply half of world production. One consequence of this concentration of supplies is that prices are likely to stay both higher and more volatile than in the past; another is that key oil supplies will be increasingly concentrated in regions where political stability is seen as questionable, heightening fears about energy security in some oil-importing nations.

Traditional oil producers have been unable to bring new supplies to market quickly enough to meet the continued growth in demand, and the tightness in the market could last for some time. In October 2007, the IEA warned that the supply crunch for oil could last into the next decade, and the agency has since undertaken a comprehensive assessment of reserves and production capabilities at the world's 400 largest oil fields. The major Middle Eastern producers, who traditionally have had few problems increasing their production rates, don't have the capacity to meet or exceed the growing demand in the short term. The major state-owned oil companies that produce much of the Middle East's easily recoverable oil are all producing at or near maximum capacity today. Saudi Aramco, for example—the state oil firm in Saudi Arabia, which owns some 20 percent of total world reserves—hopes to boost its daily production by more than 10 percent when the Khurais field comes on stream next year. Developing the field, however, required more complex engineering and construction than older Saudi wells. The project, which began in 2005, may cost as much as $15 billion and is described by company officials as one of the largest industrial projects under way in the world. Further expansions of Saudi output will be even more difficult and costly. Saudi government officials have downplayed speculation that they will raise oil output significantly in the future. Some outside analysts question Saudi Arabia's ability to continue to increase production, citing a lack of transparency in the data about Saudi reserves and depletion rates.

Oil from newly discovered reserves around the world will eventually increase supplies, but many of the big oil fields that have been discovered in recent years are in relatively remote places, and in geological formations that make extracting the oil both difficult and expensive. The biggest new find in the last 40 years, for example, was the discovery in 2000 of the Kashagan oil field, in the North Caspian Sea 50 miles off the coast of Kazakhstan, with some 13 billion barrels of recoverable oil. (To put this number in context, Saudi Arabia's reserves are estimated to be 260 billion barrels.) Oil was originally scheduled to flow in 2005, but developing the Kashagan find is turning into a cautionary tale of the technical, logistical, environmental, investment, and political hazards that await developers at the frontiers of oil production.

Temperatures at the Kashagan site range from -31°F in the winter to 104°F in the summer. The oil field lies 9,800 feet or more below the sea, which is frozen for four to five months of the year and is only about 10 feet deep at the well site. This precludes the use of traditional offshore drilling platforms, as they could be destroyed by wind-driven pack ice. Instead, the consortium developing the site had to build four artificial islands of rock, two of them surrounded by dikelike rings of ice-protection barriers. The oil reservoir has an unusually high concentration of hydrogen sulfide gas, which is fatal to humans, and thus requires elaborate safety and protection equipment (including high-tech, high-speed icebreaking getaway boats for rig workers in the event of an accident). The onshore infrastructure to support the oil field, which will include a processing facility and housing for hundreds of workers, includes 316 miles of pipelines and will require 120,000 tons of steel, 3,100 miles of electric wiring, and 195,000 cubic yards of concrete. Since the Caspian is an enclosed sea, it is more sensitive to oil spills than the open ocean, and the Kashagan field is in a nature reserve that is home to, among other species, the Caspian's caviar-producing sturgeon. Extensive controls and mechanisms have been added to capture oil discharges, but environmentalists are still skeptical.

As a result, Kashagan has been plagued by delays and cost overruns. The 2005 start-up date was pushed back first to 2008 and then, more recently, to 2010. The cost of the initial phase of development was originally put at $10 billion, but in early 2007 this was upped to $19 billion. Projected costs over the field's expected 40-year life have risen from $57 billion to $136 billion, according to Kazak officials. The government has pushed back by imposing fines on the consortium, halting development for supposed environmental infractions, enacting legislation allowing itself to abrogate its contracts, and demanding a larger share of the future profits.

The most recent discoveries of large reserves are off the coast of Brazil. In 2007, Brazil announced the discovery of the Tupi deepwater field off its southeastern coast, containing 5 to 8 billion barrels of oil. (While this is a considerable find, again, even the larger number is equal to about 3 percent of Saudi Arabia's reserves.) The oil, however, is in a formation 23,000 feet below sea level, under 7,000 feet of water, 10,000 feet of sand and rock, and another 6,000 feet of salt. Even though Petrobras, Brazil's state-owned oil company, is considered a world leader in deep-sea exploration and drilling, the project will be technologically challenging, and the earliest date that commercial production will begin is estimated to be 2013 to 2015, with full production still being several years off. In early 2008, Brazilian officials announced the discovery of another nearby deepwater field called Carioca, which they say could potentially be even larger, but which will present the same kind of challenges for drilling and production.

Oil companies are confident that additional large oil fields exist that could also add to future supplies. Large oil fields have been discovered in deepwater locations in the Gulf of Mexico, for example. One, called the Jack 2 field, is estimated to contain as much as 15 billion barrels of oil, but it is 20,000 feet under the sea floor in 7,000 feet of water. Again, the costs of recovering oil from these fields, as well as the amount of daily production they will add to world totals, are uncertain.

"UNCONVENTIONAL" OIL AND SYNFUELS

The higher oil prices go and the harder it becomes to drill conventional wells and recover oil from them, the more feasible it becomes to recover oil from unconventional sources, which contain potential oil supplies that are far larger than all known conventional oil reserves. Oil sands, for example, mostly located in Canada and Venezuela, may contain the equivalent of as much as 3.5 trillion barrels of oil—twice as much as all known reserves of conventional oil and more than a dozen times the size of the Saudi reserves.

Oil shale deposits may contain another 3 trillion barrels, and about half of these deposits are in the western United States. There is substantial environmental and political opposition to the development of these sources, but commercial production of oil from oil sands is already well under way in Canada, and oil companies are conducting pilot projects to convert shale into oil in the United States.

Energy experts have known how to make motor fuels from oil sands, oil shale, coal, and natural gas for decades. Until the price increases of the last few years, however, none of these options made economic sense except in special circumstances. At prices that seem likely in the future, some synfuels become competitive with oil, and in some cases they are already in play in the market. From an energy-security point of view, synfuels and nonconventional oil may be attractive for certain nations; from an environmental point of view, however, they present significant problems.

Oil Sands

The world has vast deposits of oil sands (also called tar sands), which contain sand or clay, water, and a very heavy, viscous form of oil. The costs of recovering and refining liquid fuels from these deposits are higher than for conventional oil, but there are no technological barriers. Oil sands are found in at least 70 nations, but three-quarters of the known reserves are located in Canada and Venezuela (where oil sands are sometimes referred to simply as "extra heavy oil"). Producing transportation fuel from oil sands is economical at oil prices that range, depending on local conditions and the technologies employed, from

EXHIBIT 3-3 **OIL SHALE MINING IN ALBERTA, CANADA**

Source: Rita Leistner/Redux

about $25 to $50 per barrel. However, open-pit mining techniques, as shown in Exhibit 3-3 (the epicenter of Canada's oil sands industry in Fort McMurray, Alberta), have led to opposition from environmentalists.

The fact that some hundreds of billions of barrels of accessible oil are located in Canada, one of the world's most stable and secure democracies, makes oil sands an attractive supply option from the energy-security perspective, particularly for the United States. Commercial development of oil sands began in the 1970s, but accelerated sharply in this decade. Canada currently produces 1.2 million barrels of oil per day from oil sands, most of it exported to the United States. Output is projected to rise to 5 million barrels per day by 2030, which would be equal to 20 percent of estimated U.S. demand. The outlook for

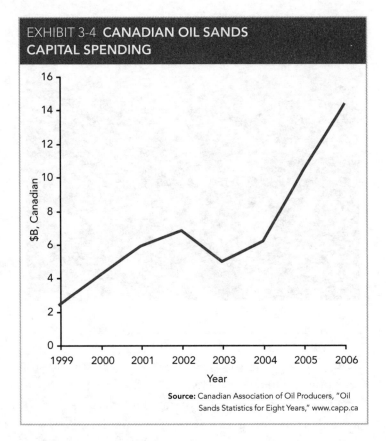

EXHIBIT 3-4 CANADIAN OIL SANDS CAPITAL SPENDING

Year

Source: Canadian Association of Oil Producers, "Oil Sands Statistics for Eight Years," www.capp.ca

developing Canadian oil sands is so promising that it has set off an investment and development boom in Alberta, the province where most of the oil sands are located. (See Exhibit 3-4 and "Canada's Unconventional Success.")

CANADA'S UNCONVENTIONAL SUCCESS by Murray Smith

Geologists, engineers, and oil and gas people have long known about Canada's oil sands. As early as the late nineteenth century, they were trying to find ways to separate oil from the sands economically and make it flow. The hunt escalated in the 1960s, and in 1967 the government of Alberta formed the Great Canadian Oil Sands Company to develop these resources. By the mid-1970s, oil was being produced, but the costs were somewhat higher than the market price of conventional crude oil, so the sense was that it wasn't going to work. When oil prices fell in the 1980s, the outlook seemed pretty bleak. A somewhat similar attempt to refine oil from oil shale in Colorado, backed by the U.S. government, was largely shut down in 1982.

Instead of letting the oil sands project die, however, the government of Alberta stepped in and put up the lion's share of money for a joint venture called the Alberta Oil Sands Technical Research Authority, along with the federal government and the private sector, which continued to fund research and development. Expenditures totaled some $800 million over a 15- to 20-year period, and the work that was done led to new technologies and tremendous innovations for recovering oil from the sands. We didn't give up, and we didn't leave, and in retrospect, it was a very shrewd investment.

Today, Alberta is producing 1.2 million barrels of oil derived from oil sands per day, most of it for export to the United States, where it supplies some 10 percent of U.S. imports. Costs of producing the oil are between $22 and $25 per barrel, which makes it very competitive at recent world oil price levels. By 2030, the Alberta Chamber of Resources estimates that oil sands production will reach 5 million barrels per day, meaning that Alberta will be able to offset the depletion of domestic U.S. supplies and help fuel economic growth. The reserves will support production for at least 150 years at 5 million barrels per day—potentially as much as 400 years.

As a resource-strong province, Alberta has always recognized the importance of environmental issues. The government ensures that there are strict emissions standards for upgraders and cokers, and that each company files an annual mine plan, a water plan, and a remediation plan. The oil and gas companies have worked with the provincial government, environmentalists, and aboriginal groups. They realize that the better they are, the more they can develop. As a result, we have seen continued improvement in the resources used, such as water, and in the carbon footprint of projects.

Development of the Alberta oil sands is the biggest engineering project on the planet today, and we are in the midst of the strongest period of economic growth ever recorded by a Canadian province. All the major oil companies are involved, and we can now offer state-of-the-art refining and processing, massive storage facilities, a world-scale petrochemical complex, a significant electricity-generation complex, and a network of transmission and marketing infrastructure to deliver value-added products to the North American and Asian markets.

Companies producing energy in Alberta continue to pioneer innovative technologies that are reducing the environmental impact and lowering the costs of production. The biggest constraint going forward may be the shortage of skilled personnel, which is affecting all energy projects. What's really needed, not just in the oil sands but in the oil and gas industry worldwide, are more engineers, more scientists, more project managers, more pipe fitters, more electricians, and more people in the trades. Skilled people are going to make a huge difference in resource extraction and energy provision over the next 30 to 40 years.

Murray Smith was appointed in January 2005 as the official representative of the Province of Alberta, Canada, to the United States of America. Prior to his diplomatic posting, he served for 12 years as a member of Alberta's Legislative Assembly. During his tenure as minister of energy (2001 to 2004), Alberta's annual oil and gas royalty revenue rose to over $9 billion, more than 20,000 wells were drilled, and over $60 billion in investment was committed to Alberta oil sands projects.

The major disadvantage of converting oil sands into motor fuel is that it worsens, on balance, global greenhouse gas emissions. In addition to the emissions that the oil and gasoline produce when they are consumed by end users, significant amounts of greenhouse gases are produced in the extraction and conversion processes. This could be overcome by adding technology to sequester and store the CO_2 produced, but this would both add to the costs and present the problem of how to dispose of and store the carbon dioxide in an environmentally acceptable and legally defensible manner. Another option would be to power the production processes with nuclear energy, which produces no greenhouse gases.

Oil Shale

Vast amounts of oil shale also exist; this is similar to oil sands in some ways, except that the oil is found in rock rather than in sand. Potential reserves are the equivalent of about three trillion barrels of oil, and about half the world's known deposits are found in the western U.S. states of Colorado, Utah, and Wyoming (mostly on government-owned land). The Rand Corporation has estimated that between 500 billion and 1.1 trillion barrels of oil are recoverable from the formation; the midpoint of that estimate, 800 billion barrels, is triple the proven reserves of Saudi Arabia.

But turning shale into oil requires even more energy and investment than the processes used to convert oil sands. Estimates of the break-even oil price for the economic production of oil from shale range from under $40 to more than $100 per barrel; in addition, the technologies for extracting oil from shale, although they have been tested in pilot programs, have not yet been proven on a commercial scale. Shale raises the same kinds of problems regarding greenhouse gases, since large amounts of energy, either fossil or nuclear, must be expended in the production of oil from shale. Royal Dutch Shell has built an advanced oil shale project in Colorado that promises to re-cover oil from shale while avoiding the environmental im-pact of open-pit mines.

Even if the technology works and environmental ob-jections can be overcome, building the infrastructure to enable large-scale commercial production would still take 12 years, according to the Rand report. Wide-scale com-mercial production would require massive investment, and would depend in part on the political environment. If oil prices continue to rise, or if the U.S. supply of im-ported oil were imperiled by geopolitical issues, oil from shale could become a viable option.

Coal and Gas

Germany developed the Fischer-Tropsch process for con-verting coal to liquid fuels in the 1920s and deployed it heavily during World War II when more conventional oil supplies were cut off. The cost of this technology made it uneconomic at postwar oil prices. South Africa's apartheid government resurrected the technology in the 1970s after oil-producing nations imposed boycotts, building coal-to-liquids and gas-to-liquids plants that are still in oper-ation today and that supply 25 percent of the nation's total liquid fuel demand.

Coal-to-liquids could make sense economically if oil prices remain at recent levels or rise further; estimates of the break-even oil-price point range from about $50 to over $100 per barrel. Developing this resource could signifi-cantly enhance energy security for countries with abun-dant coal reserves, which include the United States, China, India, and Australia. (U.S. coal reserves, in terms of energy equivalence, are larger than Saudi Arabia's oil reserves.) As with making oil from tar sands or shale, however, commercialization would require massive investment and could significantly increase greenhouse gas emissions.

Converting natural gas to liquids is simpler and less expensive, and can be cost-effective at oil prices as low as $30 per barrel. The environmental impact of gas-to-liquids plants is about the same as for oil refineries. Sasol constructed the first commercial gas-to-liquids plant outside South Africa in gas-rich Qatar in 2006 (see Exhibit 3-5); it produces 12 million barrels of oil per year, with plans to increase output to 36 million barrels per year. But since the most plentiful gas supplies tend to be in the same places as conventional oil reserves, such as the Middle East and Russia, gas-to-liquids would make little difference in the current world pattern of energy security, and would not make a significant difference in world greenhouse gas emissions.

OIL UNCERTAINTIES

The future of oil is filled with uncertainties. One important unknown, discussed in the next chapter, is how much, and how quickly, demand for transportation fuels will shift from oil to other energy sources, such as biofuels, electricity, and hydrogen. Another uncertainty, discussed in Chapter 5, is how quickly carbon sequestration and storage technology can be developed and deployed, which could pave the way for greater use of unconventional oil. Another uncertainty is how seriously national and international

EXHIBIT 3-5 GAS-TO-LIQUIDS PLANT IN QATAR

Source: Associated Press/Str

policy makers pursue legislation and regulation to limit or reduce greenhouse gas emissions.

Given the preeminent role that oil currently plays in world energy use, particularly for transportation, concerns about ensuring adequate supplies, the growth of demand, and the impact of oil prices on the world's economies will be central to energy-policy formulation to 2030 and beyond. If demand continues to grow and prices remain at or above recent record levels, pressure to exploit nonconventional sources will mount, leading to conflicts with the impetus to limit greenhouse gas emissions.

4

TRANSPORTATION: TAPERING OFF OIL

PETROLEUM PRODUCTS have reigned as the undisputed world champions of transportation fuels for the last century for three main reasons. First, gasoline and diesel oil are "energy dense" for their volume and weight, making them ideal for portable use, and at least until recently they've been relatively cheap. Second, modern internal combustion engines are compact, safe, and reliable. Finally, companies and governments around the world have invested trillions of dollars in building the infrastructure for getting petroleum-based fluids out of the ground, moving them across continents and oceans, and delivering them to consumers. The United States alone, for example, has 149 refineries, some 200,000 miles of pipelines, and 121,000 gasoline stations.

Today, for the first time since the petroleum-fueled internal combustion engine became the dominant means of propelling motor vehicles, market conditions are in place for alternatives such as biofuels, electricity, and hydrogen to become more competitive. But given the slow pace of improvement likely for greenhouse gas reduction in the transportation sector, policy initiatives to slow global warming will probably focus on the electric power industry in the near future. For transportation, rising prices and technological advances will be the main drivers for the shift away from petroleum. If prices remain near the levels reached in early 2008 or rise further, the shift will accelerate. If prices fall back much below the $60 per barrel level that many industry forecasters are using as a long-term estimate, the pace of change could slow. But both the "green" attractiveness of some new fuels and power trains and their cost advantages (as seen later in this chapter) make it likely that the shift will continue in any event.

In the meantime, myths about these alternative fuels and their potential value have clouded discussion about them. For example, one of the major myths about biofuels is that they would substantially reduce greenhouse gas emissions; another is that they will never be economically viable as a substitute for petroleum. In fact, currently available biofuels have major environmental drawbacks, and even the new generations that are currently under development may not prove to be an environmental panacea. Biofuels could, in theory, become a competitive alternative to petroleum, but serious questions about their environmental effects remain, and significant technical obstacles may take many years to overcome, during which time other alternatives may take hold.

Another myth is that a shift to electric or hydrogen cars can be accomplished in the near future. In fact, the necessary technologies are still being perfected, and the slow turnover in national fleets of cars and trucks guarantees that the impact of new fuels or new technologies will be more gradual than many environmentalists and enthusiasts would like. The hybrid vehicle (already popular) is the power train that is most likely to make fast market-share inroads, and the plug-in hybrid appears to be the best bet in the intermediate term.

Finally, there is the myth of the impact of transportation fuel. Much of the popular debate about global climate change revolves around petroleum use and the transportation sector. Yet although emissions from cars, trucks, and airplanes are the most visible and familiar source of greenhouse gas emissions for most people, the transportation sector's contribution is only 13 percent of greenhouse gas emissions caused by humans, compared to 26 percent from electricity generation. (See Exhibit 4-1.)

USING OIL MORE EFFICIENTLY

Petroleum currently supplies 94 percent of transportation energy needs, mainly in the forms of gasoline and diesel oil. Given the slow pace at which the shift to nonpetroleum fuels is happening and the current squeeze on oil supplies, one question is: will there be enough petroleum to support transportation needs in the future? The answer is yes, and one of the chief reasons (noted in Chapter 2) is that nearly half of all the oil currently being produced is used for nontransport purposes. The main nontransportation uses (or "stationary" uses) are heating for homes and commercial buildings; petrochemical feedstocks; industrial applications such as operating kilns, blast furnaces, and steam

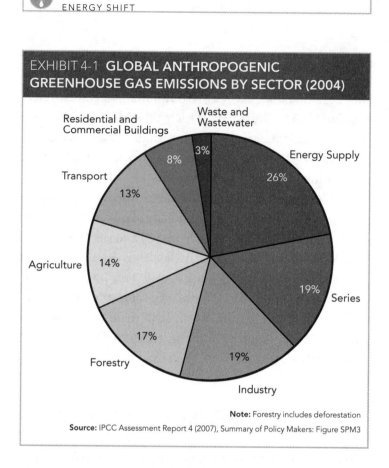

EXHIBIT 4-1 GLOBAL ANTHROPOGENIC GREENHOUSE GAS EMISSIONS BY SECTOR (2004)

Note: Forestry includes deforestation

Source: IPCC Assessment Report 4 (2007), Summary of Policy Makers: Figure SPM3

boilers; and electricity generation. Unlike transportation fuels, for which no cost-effective alternatives have been available until quite recently, there are cost-effective substitutes for oil in most stationary applications, including coal, electricity, and natural gas. The last time oil prices spiked, after the oil shocks of the 1970s, the use of petroleum for stationary applications fell significantly.

In March 2008, the world cost of electricity generation using natural gas was just 77 percent of the cost using petroleum, on average; for industrial processes, natural gas was only half as costly. If oil prices remain at or near recent levels, or rise further, much of the demand for stationary petroleum will shift to other energy sources, freeing up a greater proportion of the world oil supply for transportation uses.

Higher prices will also lead to more efficient use of petroleum in transportation. One likely effect is that cars will get lighter and smaller and will use lower-powered and more efficient engines. In Europe, high taxes on motor fuels have long encouraged the use of relatively small, energy-efficient vehicles, and higher oil prices will encourage the trend. In countries with low fuel taxes, such as the United States, the effect will be more dramatic. Sales of larger cars and sport-utility vehicles in the United States have already fallen dramatically. Again, the experience after the oil shocks of the 1970s provides a historical precedent. Rising prices, combined with federal fuel-mileage standards, led to a 20 percent decline in both the average size of vehicles and their horsepower-to-weight ratio between 1972 and 1982.

Higher petroleum prices will also encourage the greater use of diesel engines, which are inherently more efficient than gasoline engines, providing both significantly better fuel mileage and lower greenhouse gas emissions. Until the 1990s, diesels were unable to match the performance characteristics of gasoline engines, especially in acceleration, and they were also noisier. In the early 1990s, European automakers began introducing technologically advanced turbo diesel designs that significantly improved performance, and in 2000, improved fuel-injection systems made further strides. From 1985 to 2005, for example, acceleration for a typical model improved by nearly 50 percent, and European automakers gained publicity by winning

EXHIBIT 4-2 AN AUDI R10 DIESEL WINS THE 2006 LE MANS 24-HOUR RACE

Source: Andre Durand/AFP/Getty Images

major auto races, such as the 24 hours of Le Mans, with diesel-powered race cars (see Exhibit 4-2). Today's automotive diesel engines, as a result, have performance fully comparable to gasoline engines, yet are more fuel-efficient. As a result, diesels have made the biggest gains in Europe, where high fuel taxes reward that efficiency.

Although the purchase price of diesel autos can be as much as 25 percent higher than that of equivalent gasoline models, their superior fuel efficiency, coupled with the tax advantage, give them a lower total cost of ownership over the vehicle's lifetime. Diesels as a percentage of total new car sales in Western European countries rose steadily from 22 percent in 1996 to 51 percent in 2006, in close correlation with the improvements in performance. In some countries, diesel penetration rates in the new car market are more than 66 percent. From 1995 to 2005, the demand

EXHIBIT 4-3 **A GAS-ELECTRIC HYBRID AT AN ECO-FRIENDLY GAS STATION IN LOS ANGELES**

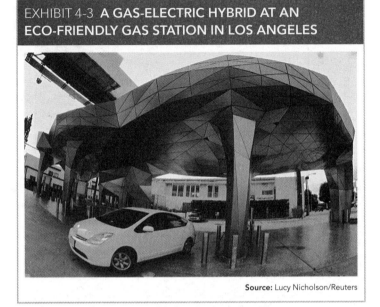

Source: Lucy Nicholson/Reuters

for gasoline in Western Europe declined at an average annual rate of 1.9 percent, while the demand for diesel oil rose at a rate of 4.4 percent. Auto companies have recently begun to promote modern diesel power trains in the U.S. market as well.

The biggest recent innovation in power trains is the hybrid car, which uses a gasoline engine in combination with a battery and an electric motor to increase fuel efficiency. Hybrid sales have been modest to date. In the United States, hybrids currently make up only about 3 percent of the new-car market and a tiny percentage of the total U.S. vehicle fleet. Market shares are even smaller elsewhere. But hybrids have proved popular with consumers in some regions and are gaining greater acceptance, and sales are expected to rise sharply in the coming years (see Exhibits 4-3 and 4-4). At recent high gasoline

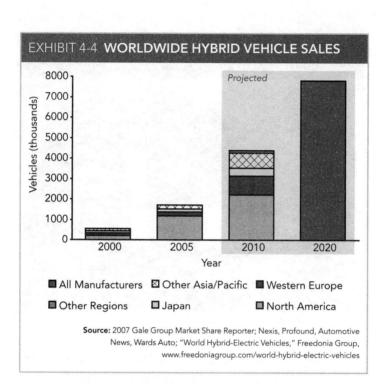

EXHIBIT 4-4 **WORLDWIDE HYBRID VEHICLE SALES**

■ All Manufacturers ☒ Other Asia/Pacific ■ Western Europe
■ Other Regions ☐ Japan ■ North America

Source: 2007 Gale Group Market Share Reporter; Nexis, Profound, Automotive News, Wards Auto; "World Hybrid-Electric Vehicles," Freedonia Group, www.freedoniagroup.com/world-hybrid-electric-vehicles

prices, hybrids are cost-effective (the fuel savings offset their higher prices compared to equivalent conventional cars), and consumers have shown some willingness to pay a small premium for them. Continued high oil prices should drive market share significantly in the future. Toyota's Prius model, the market leader (and also a top performer in fuel-efficiency comparisons) is in its third generation, and many other models are being offered by Toyota and other automakers. Given current trends in performance improvement, hybrids are likely to achieve parity with conventional power trains in total cost of ownership by 2015, even at much lower oil prices.

The chief disadvantage of hybrids is that their fuel-efficiency advantage comes in stop-and-go driving (the design uses energy produced by braking to recharge the car's battery), so that they are most likely to be popular with those living in cities and suburbs, and are not price-competitive in places where more driving is done on highways. Diesel hybrids are more likely to gain market share in Europe, where they would enjoy the same tax advantage as conventional diesel cars. European automakers have been skeptical about the market-share possibilities of hybrids, but are now beginning to offer hybrid models.

The next step toward greater fuel efficiency is the plug-in hybrid. In these power trains, the gasoline/electricity equation of the conventional hybrid is flipped over, and the car uses its electric motor and battery for the bulk of its energy, with the gasoline (or diesel) engine providing auxiliary power. The battery is recharged by plugging it into a conventional electric outlet.

Plug-in hybrids, like the modified Toyota Prius at the National Renewable Energy Laboratory in Golden, Colorado, in Exhibit 4-5, are still being tested: Toyota and General Motors have prototypes on the road, and other automakers are following suit. The chief concern with plug-ins is whether battery technology is moving fast enough to make them attractive to large numbers of consumers. Since they rely heavily on electricity, the key to their range and performance is how much power the battery can store. Battery technology, however, seems to be moving forward relatively quickly; battery costs, for example, are currently being cut in half every seven years, compared to a 1.3 percent rate for internal combustion engines, according to a Booz & Company analysis of the scientific literature. And there are many companies competing to bring the next innovation to market. Better, cheaper batteries could make

EXHIBIT 4-5 MODIFIED PLUG-IN TOYOTA PRIUS

Source: David Zalubowski/ Associated Press

plug-in hybrids competitive with conventional cars on a total-cost-of-ownership basis sometime in the next decade, and, as in the case of conventional hybrids, automakers will bring them to market even before they achieve cost parity.

If the plug-in hybrid succeeds in the marketplace, it will represent a major turning point in transportation fuel history: since most of the energy it uses comes from electricity, the point at which fuel is used to produce energy shifts from the vehicle itself to the electric grid, which in turn can be powered by a wide variety of fuels. The cost of the electric power used in a hybrid, according to a 2006 study by the State of California, can be as low as $0.75 for the equivalent of one gallon of gasoline.

Plug-in hybrids, however, do raise questions and pose challenges for infrastructure. Since city drivers would be among the consumers most likely to purchase plug-in hybrids, how will people who live in apartments plug in their cars at night? Will we need to retrofit parking meters with metered electricity outlets? Some cities, notably London, have already introduced street recharging stations for electric cars. But deploying them on a mass scale would be a large undertaking. These questions will need to be sorted out, but plug-in hybrids could begin to be widely available within the next few years.

MOVING BEYOND OIL

Biofuels

The development of biofuels such as ethanol and biodiesel has been one of the major phenomena of the energy shift so far, marking the first time that alternatives to petroleum have become viable as transportation fuels. Biofuels use renewable resources and promote energy security, but much of the initial enthusiasm about them over the last few years was based on a myth: that substituting biofuels for petroleum would substantially reduce greenhouse gas emissions. At first glance, biofuels do seem to have a much smaller carbon footprint than oil, since the feedstock crops used in their production (like all crops) absorb CO_2 as they grow and, in effect, release it into the atmosphere when the biofuels are combusted—a process that can be repeated without adding to the total volume of CO_2. Indeed, studies such as the International Energy Agency's 2004 *Biofuels for Transport* report indicated that the "well-to-wheel" greenhouse gas savings from biofuels could range from 20 percent with corn ethanol to 80 percent or higher with sugarcane ethanol or cellulosic ethanol (produced from grass, plant residues, and woody crops).

However, these well-to-wheel savings failed to take into account the impact of farming land that had been, or would otherwise revert to, grassland or forest. Clearing land to convert forest or grassland into energy crops results in a substantial deposit of carbon dioxide into the atmosphere. The magnitude of that deposit depends on the type of property. For example, clear-cutting and burning a forest releases more carbon dioxide than harvesting grass. And studies recently published in *Science* found that when this initial carbon dioxide deposit is taken into account, depending on the type of land used for agriculture and the type of crop grown, ethanol's contribution to greenhouse gas emissions could be equal to that of petroleum in anywhere from a couple of decades to a few centuries. That said, some emerging biofuel technologies, such as cellulosic and algaeic, require less active cultivation of land. Consequently, peering further into the future, the environmental hope for biofuels is not a complete chimera.

A second myth about biofuels is that they are not economically viable as a substitute for petroleum. In fact, while the breakeven costs for different biofuel technologies vary significantly, sugarcane ethanol in Brazil is already commercially viable, and Brazil is second only to the United States in ethanol production (see Exhibit 4-6). Introduced in the 1970s, cane ethanol was nurtured as an infant industry and backed by public subsidies for many years, largely because of the government's desire to achieve energy independence and to conserve foreign currency reserves. Brazil's government-financed new ethanol plants, like the one pictured in Exhibit 4-7, directed the state-

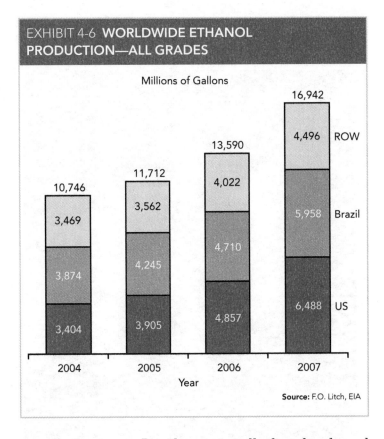

EXHIBIT 4-6 WORLDWIDE ETHANOL PRODUCTION—ALL GRADES

Millions of Gallons

Source: F.O. Litch, EIA

owned oil company Petrobras to install ethanol tanks and pumps throughout the country, and mandated that carmakers design and manufacture cars that could run on pure ethanol.

About a decade ago, Brazil phased out the subsidies, but since there was a thriving, efficient cane ethanol industry in place, car manufacturers had to find an inexpensive way to make vehicles that could burn both fuels. The answer was the flex-fuel engine, based on a simple invention by a Brazilian engineer and pioneered by Volkswagen, which can burn pure gasoline, pure ethanol, or any mixture of the

EXHIBIT 4-7 **AN ETHANOL PROCESSING PLANT IN BRAZIL**

Source: Ricardo Azoury/Redux

two. Today all major automakers offer flex-fuel power trains in Brazil, and they command 85 percent of the new-car market. Cane ethanol supplies a significant portion of Brazil's automotive fuel pool based solely on its economic merits. Thanks to the large number of flex-fuel vehicles, consumers can opt for whichever fuel is cheaper, which ultimately depends on the relative prices of crude oil and sugar.

Globally, corn ethanol is still more expensive than petroleum unless oil prices are above $130 per barrel. Cellulosic ethanol, although still in the early stage of development, will probably break even with petroleum when the former is at around $55 per barrel, without government incentives—below the long-term projections of $60 or more that oil companies often use.

Other potential innovations include biobutanol, which is less corrosive than ethanol, is easier to mix with gasoline, and can be easily transported via pipeline (unlike ethanol, which must be transported by truck or train). Production costs in 2008 are too high to make it competitive with gasoline or ethanol, although several companies, including BP and DuPont, are working to bring it to market. One of the most exciting future-generation biofuels is biodiesel made with algae as a feedstock. Although algae-based biodiesel is still in the experimental and start-up phase—certainly several years away from commercialization and many years away from potential widespread adoption—many energy practitioners consider it among the most promising ideas on the technological horizon. Algae, which occur naturally in everything from swimming pools to oceans, can be used to make oil, and could theoretically be grown in pipes in a factorylike setting, avoiding the land-use problems of most biofuels. Better still, algae can be fed a diet rich in carbon dioxide, the greenhouse gas most responsible for global warming. Thus, by locating an algae biodiesel plant next to a coal plant, producers could feed the carbon to the algae and get two turns of energy generation from the same amount of carbon emissions.

Today, biofuels production accounts for less than 1 percent of total global fuel demand, but if agricultural improvements continue apace or technological break-throughs occur, biofuels could, in theory, eventually supply a significant portion of transportation fuel needs. A recent Booz & Company study, prepared by Senior Partner William Jackson for the World Economic Forum, found that depending on the price of oil, biofuels could supply as much as 20 to 30 million barrels per day globally by 2030. Over the longer term, however, the most important competitors for both petroleum and biofuels may be nonliquid fuels that have the advantage of producing no emissions on the road—electricity and hydrogen. Both are still in the developmental stages as mass-production technologies.

Electricity

The next step in shifting transport power off the road and onto the electric grid is the all-electric car. There are already electric cars in operation in specific markets around the world. A Norwegian company, Think Global, sells small electric cars in Europe and plans to introduce them in the United States in 2009. Backed by U.S. venture capital firms, the company plans to offer a second-generation electric car in 2011 that will have a range of 125 or more miles between rechargings—and, the company promises, performance comparable to that of conventional cars. Renault-Nissan has a major project in place, beginning in 2011, to produce all-electric cars for Israel. Another firm, the REVA Electric Car Company in Bangalore, India, offers a small, basic model, shown in Exhibit 4-8, in India and in the United Kingdom. At the other end of the automotive spectrum is a $98,000 two-seat, high-performance roadster being tested by Tesla Motors, a Silicon Valley start-up, shown in Exhibit 4-9.

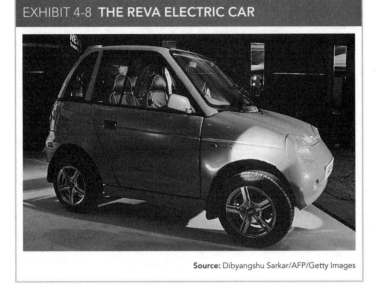

EXHIBIT 4-8 **THE REVA ELECTRIC CAR**

Source: Dibyangshu Sarkar/AFP/Getty Images

All the problems with battery efficiency, range, and infrastructure facing plug-in hybrids are present for all-electric cars as well, and are even more critical since there is no petroleum-fueled auxiliary power to fall back on. Major automakers have built all-electric concept cars and prototypes since the 1960s, and they are continuing to build and test new ones. Several companies have plans to introduce new models over the next several years.

Hydrogen

Like electric cars, hydrogen cars use energy that is pro-duced elsewhere and stored on board the vehicle. One advantage of hydrogen cars over plug-in hybrids and all-electric cars is that they can be refueled rather than recharged, which makes them better suited and more con-venient for long-distance driving. In the same way that an

EXHIBIT 4-9 **THE TESLA ROADSTER**

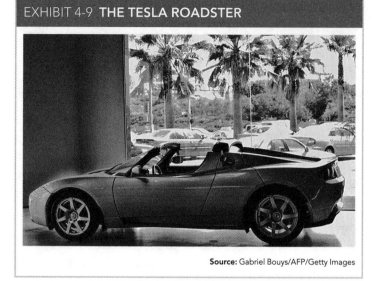

Source: Gabriel Bouys/AFP/Getty Images

all-electric car's performance depends on its batteries, however, the practicality of a hydrogen-powered car is determined in large part by the energy capacity of hydrogen. The main problem is that hydrogen gas must be compressed or liquefied to store enough energy to equal the range of conventional power trains, significantly complicating the design of the vehicle, as well as raising safety concerns. And the development of cost-effective, practical, and robust hydrogen fuel cells—the devices that convert the energy in the hydrogen into electricity to power the vehicle—is still at a relatively early stage, although many companies are vying to produce robust designs, and significant investments have been made in fuel research and development. The main problem is that hydrogen gas must be compressed or liquefied to store enough energy to equal the range of conventional power trains, significantly complicating the design and manufacture of the fuel cells.

Unlike electric cars, which can tap into the existing power grid to deliver energy to their batteries, distributing hydrogen will require new infrastructure. Automakers have plans to phase in hydrogen cars regionally, building the distribution infrastructure incrementally, and have concluded that the costs will not be prohibitive. Several automakers have hydrogen prototypes on the road. General Motors, for example, will test 100 of its new Equinox sport-utility vehicles with families in 2008. But going from testing prototypes to full-scale production is likely to take 10 years.

One other nonpetroleum transport fuel, compressed natural gas (CNG), has received substantial publicity, particularly in the United States. Although in use for many decades, vehicles powered by CNG have never become popular, largely because the energy density of CNG is only 21 percent that of gasoline, requiring large fuel tanks and severely limiting the vehicles' driving range. Also, widespread adoption of CNG would require the same kind of infrastructure investments as hydrogen, and—unlike electricity or hydrogen—still produce greenhouse gases on the road. It thus seems unlikely to play a major role in the energy shift.

UNSCRAMBLING THE ALTERNATIVES

Over the next decade, automakers—and consumers—will begin to determine how practical, cost-effective, and appealing all-electric and hydrogen cars turn out to be; in the meantime, we're likely to see an increasingly diverse mix of vehicles on the road. Conventional diesels may gain market share, both in Europe, where they have already had great success, and in other regions. (See "The View from Detroit" for an auto industry perspective.) Biofuels, small percentages of which are currently mixed with fossil fuels, will continue to increase in volume, but the penetration of vehicles running on pure biofuels is likely to be slow, except in specific nations like Brazil and regions like the U.S. Midwest. The conventional hybrid seems the most likely new power train to gain market share in the short term, especially for environmentally conscious consumers in urban and suburban areas. At some point within the next several years, plug-in hybrids will begin to become more commonplace, although their success will depend in part on advances in battery technology. Over the medium term, the plug-in hybrid appears to be the most promising new automotive platform for shifting away from petroleum.

Longer term, all-electric and hydrogen cars seem to be the chief contenders for dominance in a carbon-constrained world, with electric cars having the early advantage. Moving to new generations of fuels on a mass scale, however, presents a serious coordination problem for the energy and auto industries. The investments required to produce alternative fuels on this scale are large, and are difficult for individual companies to undertake, given the uncertainties concerning future oil prices and future government regulation and taxation. Energy companies are hesitant to make large, long-term investments to develop new fuel sources and build new distribution facilities unless they have some assurance about future environmental and tax policies that could affect demand, and their investment horizons are often 20 years or longer. Automakers, on the other hand, are hesitant to make investments in new power trains and vehicles given the uncertainties about which fuel sources will be favored, and their time horizons are more like 3 to 10 years. This asymmetry creates an awkward dynamic in the market, and substantial uncertainty for companies.

Furthermore, changing to alternative fuels may require significant modification—or even replacement—of the existing supply and distribution infrastructure, which will also require large investments. There are also long lags between action and results in the transportation sector: turnover in national fleets of cars and trucks takes about 15 years, suggesting that the impact of new fuels or new technologies on greenhouse gas emissions will be slow and gradual. In addition, the older, less fuel-efficient vehicles that are replaced don't disappear. Most of them are sold in the used-car market, in some cases migrating from more prosperous countries to less prosperous ones. Outdated cars from Europe will make their way into Central Asia; outdated cars from the United States will show up in Latin America. In any case, their emissions remain the same.

Under the most optimistic assumptions about all these fuel sources and technologies, it's a safe bet that even a decade or more hence, most vehicles in use will still be burning fossil fuels, and a great many will be powered by nothing else. As a result, significant changes in greenhouse gas emissions are unlikely to come from the transportation sector—certainly not within the next 10 to 15 years. In addition, even if electricity or hydrogen eventually supplants gasoline and diesel, this will not eliminate greenhouse gas emissions: to the extent that the electricity or hydrogen that power these vehicles is produced from fossil fuels, their adoption will merely shift the emissions from the vehicle to the power-generation sector, which is the subject of the next chapter.

THE VIEW FROM DETROIT   by Larry Burns

Over the last 10 years, General Motors has been seeking to put technologies in place that will allow us to diversify the energy used in automobiles. We saw the enormous growth potential for our industry as economies like China, India, Brazil, Russia, and Korea developed, but at the same time it was clear to us that challenges like energy, the environment, safety, and congestion were all going to have a major impact. We wanted to find a way to manage through what we saw was going to be a significant transformation of the industry.

Ethanol was very attractive to us, since it is a liquid fuel that burns in an internal combustion engine with lower carbon dioxide emissions and can be produced locally. We have had great success in Brazil, where we have been building flex-fuel vehicles that can burn either ethanol or gasoline. Three years ago we launched a major campaign for ethanol in the United States, introducing flex-fuel engines that can burn E85 ethanol, originally in our larger sport-utility vehicles. We built 1 million flex-fuel vehicles in 2007, and we currently have over 3.5 million on the road. If every auto company did what GM has committed to do with E85, and if the United States produced enough ethanol for flex-fuel vehicles to run on it all the time, we would save four times as much petroleum as with the recent corporate average fuel efficiency (CAFE) legislation. The economics of cellulosic ethanol look very good going forward. In the short term, there's nothing else out there that can have as great an impact on the CO_2 emissions of cars or that can do as much to reduce our dependence on petroleum.

We believe, however, that we are in an industry where regulators won't relax until we truly have zero-emission vehicles. This is true not just in the United States or in California, but also in Europe and elsewhere. So the goal became to produce a drive train that doesn't emit anything. Ten years ago, we saw two pathways, electric and hydrogen power, and we have pursued both. In 2002 we introduced a new concept for drive trains, in which the car is driven by electric motors that are digitally and electronically controlled, and that can be energized with either electricity or hydrogen.

We have built demonstration models of this car, called the Sequel (as in the sequel to the first hundred years of the auto industry), powered by a hydrogen fuel cell and meeting all federal highway safety standards. It stores eight kilograms of hydrogen, has a lithium-ion battery for regenerative braking, and has electronic air conditioning. It is the most technologically advanced vehicle ever built. In 2007 we drove one of these cars 300 miles—totally emission free—from Rochester to New York City on a single tank of hydrogen. The hydrogen was created from electricity generated at Niagara Falls, so it was green energy. Today we are test marketing 100 Chevrolet Equinox fuel cell vehicles with families around the

United States, and we will collect the market data on their overall experience.

Since we are interested in energy diversity, we wanted to find a way to use electricity from the grid as well, and last year we unveiled a new extended-range all-electric car, the Chevrolet Volt, that can travel more than 200 miles without recharging. It has captured the imagination of a lot of people, and we have committed to putting it into production. We are also introducing hybrid vehicles at the rate of one new model per quarter for the next four years. In addition, in gasoline engines, we were the first North American auto company to have homogeneous charge-compression ignition rather than spark ignition. This combines the cleanliness and affordability of gasoline engines with the fuel efficiency and emissions advantages of diesels.

These are very different solutions, and we believe that the consumer will have something to say about which are the most attractive. Our aim is to position ourselves in all technologies with respect to the future of propulsion systems. Whether it is hydrogen, electricity, biofuels, or petroleum, we are trying to drive the diversity so that we can take advantage of the huge growth potential in this industry.

Larry Burns is vice president of General Motors Research & Development and Strategic Planning. In this post, he oversees GM's advanced technology programs, innovation programs, and corporate strategy. He is a member of GM's Automotive Strategy Board and Automotive Product Board.

COAL'S QUESTIONABLE FUTURE

WHILE THE TRANSPORTATION sector gets much of the attention in discussions about the future of energy, a larger proportion of energy is used in "stationary" applications, which include heating (both residential and commercial), industrial processes, feedstocks for petrochemicals, and electricity production—the biggest and fastest growing category. How the world fuels stationary energy uses in general, and electric power generation in particular, will play a leading role in the energy shift, and will be crucial to the world's success in combating climate change. We begin with the outlook for coal, the most problematic major energy source.

Coal is the largest source of fuel for the electric power industry, but it is also a leading producer of greenhouse gases. If the energy shift is to have any hope of slowing the process of global warming, the world will need to either wean itself away from burning coal or invest in new technologies to clean up coal emissions. Because of this dynamic, the coal mining and power-generation industries today exist in an environment of huge uncertainty. As we will see in the next two chapters, coal faces competitive pressure in the short term from natural gas and, to a lesser extent, in the long term from both nuclear energy and renewable energy sources such as wind, biomass, and solar power.

Nearly 1 trillion tons of recoverable coal reserves exist—enough to support current production levels for some 147 years, more than a century longer than the reserves of conventional oil are forecast to last. Better still, some of the most plentiful coal reserves are located in countries that are major energy users and are concerned about their dependence on imported fuels, such as the United States, China, and India. Coal has many virtues as a fuel source: it is energy-dense and its production and supply chains are extensive and efficient. More important, it is also relatively cheap compared to other forms of energy, especially given the recent prices for oil and natural gas. Coal currently provides some 25 percent of the world's primary energy supply and 40 percent of world electricity generation, and in theory could supply much more. It can even be converted, as noted in Chapter 3, into high-quality synfuel substitutes for gasoline, diesel oil, and aviation fuel that would be competitive with petroleum at recent record oil prices, using existing, proven technology.

But the catch—and it's a big one—is that burning coal creates negative environmental by-products: in addition to producing noxious chemicals like nitrogen and sulfur oxides, coal produces more carbon dioxide emissions per unit of energy output than any other fuel—about twice as much, for example, as natural gas. Currently, coal ranks second to oil as a producer of CO_2 emissions, but coal consumption is rising faster than oil consumption, and by 2030, coal will likely take over the number one spot, producing 43 percent of all energy-related CO_2, compared to 36 percent for oil and 21 percent for natural gas, according to the Energy Information Administration. The current growth trend suggests that coal's abundance and low costs are outweighing its environmental drawbacks, especially in the developing world.

Given the shift in public and political perceptions about the dangers of global warming, policy efforts to significantly reduce the increase in CO_2 emissions will intensify. These are likely to take the form of "cap-and-trade" systems that put a market price on greenhouse gas emissions and create tradable allowances, such as the system instituted by the European Union in 2005. A similar approach is expected to be enacted in the United States in 2009–2010. At the international level, the United Nations' 1997 Kyoto Accord, which set modest goals for greenhouse gas reductions, will likely be superseded by a more stringent treaty in the next few years, perhaps as early as November 2009, when government representatives from 170 nations, parties to the U.N. Framework Convention on Climate, meet in Copenhagen.

Efforts to reduce greenhouse gas emissions are likely to place the heaviest burden on coal, especially on coal-fired power plants. The main reason is that power generation (examined in detail in Chapter 8) is the sector in which major emissions reductions are feasible over relatively short time horizons by governmental emissions controls. In transportation, another major sector producing greenhouse gases, emissions reductions take longer to produce results because of both the current lack of alternative energy sources on a mass scale and the slow turnover of world vehicle fleets. In addition, studies by Booz & Company suggest that the total costs of reducing CO_2 emissions in electricity generation are significantly lower than those of trying to limit emissions in transportation.

The extension and wider application of cap-and-trade systems to reduce greenhouse gas emissions would have powerful effects on the future of coal. One effect would be to shift demand from coal to other fuels, especially to natural gas; another would be to speed the development and deployment of carbon capture and sequestration (CCS) technologies to remove CO_2 emissions as coal is combusted and store them in underground reservoirs. More broadly, coal gasification—similar to the technology used in coal-to-liquids production—could offer a potential pathway for using coal without the need for expensive postcombustion separation. This would be economic, however, only if natural gas prices were to rise significantly from recent levels.

SUPPLY SECURITY

Nearly 80 percent of the world's recoverable coal reserves are found in six nations, with the greatest concentrations being in the United States, Russia, and China (see Exhibit 5-1). The United States, in fact, is sometimes called "the Saudi Arabia of coal," since it possesses a greater share of world coal reserves than Saudi Arabia's share of petroleum.

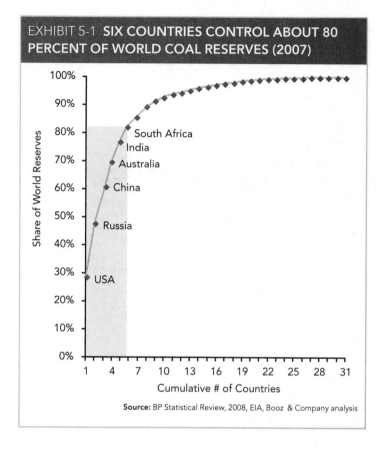

EXHIBIT 5-1 **SIX COUNTRIES CONTROL ABOUT 80 PERCENT OF WORLD COAL RESERVES (2007)**

Share of World Reserves (y-axis): 0% to 100%

South Africa
India
Australia
China
Russia
USA

Cumulative # of Countries (x-axis): 1, 4, 7, 10, 13, 16, 19, 22, 25, 28, 31

Source: BP Statistical Review, 2008, EIA, Booz & Company analysis

For the most part, coal is mined and consumed locally because of its high transport costs (see Exhibit 5-2). The U.S. market remains largely self-contained, as do those in China and India. Countries such as Australia, Indonesia, Russia, and South Africa are significant exporters. Several countries depend on coal for very large percentages of their total energy needs, including South Africa (76 percent), China (65 percent), and India (52 percent). The world distribution of reserves makes coal an important energy source from a strategic point of view for countries that are

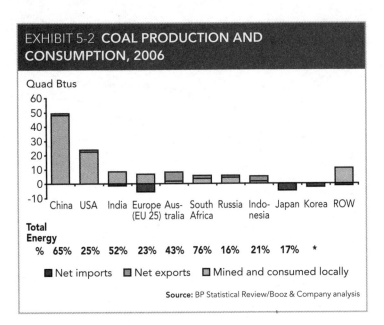

EXHIBIT 5-2 **COAL PRODUCTION AND CONSUMPTION, 2006**

Quad Btus

	China	USA	India	Europe (EU 25)	Australia	South Africa	Russia	Indonesia	Japan	Korea	ROW
Total Energy %	65%	25%	52%	23%	43%	76%	16%	21%	17%	*	

■ Net imports ■ Net exports ■ Mined and consumed locally

Source: BP Statistical Review/Booz & Company analysis

concerned about having reliable energy supplies that are unaffected by political or military instability. For countries with large reserves, coal provides both long-term security, or resource availability, and also short-term security, in that it is not subject to sudden supply interruptions.

GROWTH AND GREENHOUSE GASES

Until recently, demand for coal was growing slowly. From 1985 to 2002, worldwide demand was growing at an average annual rate of just 1 percent. Since then, however, demand growth has risen sharply, in large part because of the surge in demand from China for power generation and heavy industry (see Exhibit 5-3). Also noteworthy is the change in the trend of demand after 2002 in the former Soviet Union countries and the EU, where demand had

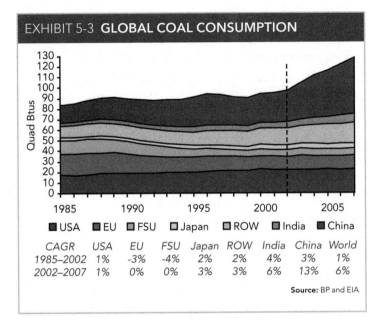

EXHIBIT 5-3 **GLOBAL COAL CONSUMPTION**

CAGR	USA	EU	FSU	Japan	ROW	India	China	World
1985–2002	1%	-3%	-4%	2%	2%	4%	3%	1%
2002–2007	1%	0%	0%	3%	3%	6%	13%	6%

Source: BP and EIA

been falling before 2002 but has been growing since. In fact, other than in the United States, where coal demand has been flat, all regions show some increase in demand growth. Despite sharp increases since 2002, coal prices have risen less than oil and gas prices. Historically, coal prices have been both lower and less volatile than oil or gas prices, because of both the abundance of supplies and the more regional, dispersed nature of coal markets.

As recently as early 2007, the combination of coal's cost advantage and energy-security attributes had seemingly set the stage for a large-scale renaissance in the use of coal for electricity generation (detailed in Chapter 8), but environmental opposition has delayed or derailed many of the plans for new coal plants, especially in Europe and the United States (although construction of coal plants has continued in developing nations, particularly China, which is adding one new plant, on average, per week). One reason for the abrupt reversal is the uncertainty about future regulatory or tax initiatives that would assess a charge for CO_2 emissions and, as a result, uncertainty about the new plants' future profitability. (See "Coal at a Crossroads.") Another reason is intense opposition from environmentalists and local governmental entities, which has gained force as concerns about global warming have become more widespread.

COAL AT A CROSSROADS by Michael J. Quillen

The biggest public perception problem that coal suffers from right now is related to concerns about global warming. This perception has gotten much more negative in the recent past, and it has resulted in the cancellation of many plans that had been made for new coal-fired power plants in the United States. Despite that, we will probably see a dozen or so new coal plants come online by 2010. Local politicians are not really standing up and fighting for new plants, and neither are the utility companies. A big reason is that no one knows what the ground rules are going to be regarding carbon pricing—whether we're going to have a cap-and-trade system, a carbon tax, or something else. This uncertainty has a chilling effect on capital expansions.

The problems for coal aren't going to be resolved until we get some sound energy policies that allow the utilities, the producers, and, particularly, the financial community to know what the rules are going to be. We have seen a big run-up in the costs of components of new power plants like steel and concrete; these are all billion-dollar projects today. Utilities are not going to ask their shareholders for that kind of money, and no bank is going to lend you a billion dollars, when a future change in regulation could make the plant uneconomic.

The pendulum may be swinging too far. The only three choices for uninterruptible base load power in the United States today are coal, natural gas, and nuclear energy. The future price of natural gas is uncertain, and it could easily rise much higher than it is today. Nuclear power has its own set of issues, and faces the same kind of cost run-ups that coal plants face.

At some point economics will come into play, and the result could be a big rise in people's power bills. That would have its own consequences. You could see a groundswell for building more coal-fired electricity generation capacity, and if that happens, politicians will react to it.

To address the environmental concerns about coal, we need a large-scale program to test carbon capture and sequestration. It's been done at a very minimal level at this stage and there is a lot of optimism from an engineering standpoint that it will work. Larger-scale projects will add to our knowledge, and technologically, we are going to know a lot more in the next two to three years.

But making carbon sequestration and storage work from a commercial point of view will be much more complicated. There are some huge legal liability and logistical issues that need to be dealt with, concerning how you transport and store the CO_2. We will probably see some plants built in a 10-year time frame in locations where the conditions are right for storing CO_2. It will probably be more like 10 or 15 years, however, before these issues are all resolved to the point where carbon capture and sequestration can be done on a commercial scale.

Michael J. Quillen is chairman and chief executive officer of Alpha Natural Resources. He has more than 30 years' experience in the coal business, starting as an engineer. Alpha, with revenues of more than $2.5 billion, is a leading central Appalachian coal producer that also has significant operations in northern Appalachia, producing both steam coal used in electricity generation and metallurgical coal used primarily in the steelmaking process. Alpha has 38 active underground mines, 27 active surface mines, and 10 preparation plants located throughout Virginia, West Virginia, Kentucky, and Pennsylvania.

Nevertheless, future growth in coal consumption is expected to be strong. In the Energy Information Administration's reference case estimates, coal consumption grows at a 2.2 percent annual rate, on average, from 2004 to 2030, for a total increase of 74 percent. Non-OECD Asia accounts for 85 percent of that growth. This projected growth path for coal consumption, however, is on a collision course with the policy imperative of reducing greenhouse gas emissions. Coal is currently producing 39 percent of the world's total greenhouse gas emissions, and its share will rise to 43 percent by 2030 in the EIA reference case. At that point, coal alone would be producing more than 18 billion metric tons of CO_2 per year—about two-thirds as much as emissions from all sources today. Thus, any plan to constrain greenhouse gas emissions into the atmosphere cannot succeed unless coal consumption slows or emissions from coal are reduced or stored.

The technology to control greenhouse gas emissions from coal combustion—carbon capture and sequestration (CCS)—exists, and several small- to medium-sized demonstration plants are operating in Europe and the United States, proving that the basic technology is feasible. So far, however, CCS has not been tested on a commercial scale. The next hurdle is what to do with the CO_2. The plan is to pump it into geological formations deep underground, where it will be stored—in theory—permanently. The clouded outlook for CCS is exemplified by the fate of FutureGen, a public-private alliance between the U.S. Department of Energy and 12 power-generation and mining companies from Australia, China, the United Kingdom, and the United States. Funded with $1.2 billion from the U.S. government and $400 million from private-sector members, FutureGen planned to build a commercially scaled power plant (pictured in Exhibit 5-4) with CCS technology to capture CO_2 and store it permanently one mile below the plant site in Illinois. The project was launched with great fanfare in 2003; the site was selected in late 2007, and operations were set to begin in 2012, but the U.S. government suddenly canceled its support in January 2008, after costs rose far above the original estimates.

Even if CCS technology works as envisioned, current estimates of the costs vary, ranging from $80 to $100 per ton of CO_2 sequestered. Making this work on a mass scale would also be a vast undertaking given the quantities of

EXHIBIT 5-4 **THE CANCELED FUTUREGEN POWER PLANT**

Source: Associated Press/U.S. Department of Energy.

CO_2 involved. A recent study by the Massachusetts Institute of Technology, *The Future of Coal*, estimated that the 1.5 billion tons of CO_2 produced by U.S. coal-fired power plants is equal to one-third of the total volume of natural gas transported per year by U.S. gas pipelines.

POLICY FOR GREENHOUSE GAS REDUCTION

The future of coal depends crucially on the future of greenhouse gas regulation. Policy efforts to change the mix and use of fuels to reduce greenhouse gases have been in the works for more than a decade, but are only now beginning to affect markets powerfully. At the regional and national level, there are three ways for nations to limit greenhouse gas emissions: direct regulation, taxation, and cap-and-trade systems. Direct regulation, or "command and control," is impractical in most modern market economies. Carbon taxes have been adopted by some counties, notably Sweden, Finland, the Netherlands, and Norway. One advantage is that governments can set a specific tax rate per ton for CO_2 emissions. But the most practical approach appears to be the cap-and-trade system, in which the government caps the total amount of emissions, then issues permits allowing companies specific amounts of emissions. Companies that reduce their emissions are given credits, or allowances, that can be traded, and these credits can be bought by companies that are exceeding their permit levels. By reducing the overall level of permits and credits over time, the government can reduce total emissions of CO_2. If the system is designed correctly, the cost of tradable credits will equal the cost per ton of CO_2 that the government deems appropriate, so the system can thus accomplish the same goals as a direct tax. The cap-and-trade approach gives the government flexibility in targeting emissions reductions for specific industries, and gives companies more flexibility in compliance.

The European Union set up the largest regional cap-and-trade system in 2005 as part of its overall policy for climate change. The EU Emissions Trading Scheme, which covers 27 member countries today, aims for a 20 percent reduction in CO_2 from 1990 levels by 2020. The first phase of the program, which ran from 2005 to 2007, was generally viewed as unsuccessful. Countries set caps at excessively high levels and issued too many permits and allowances. As a result, the trading value of allowances, which initially rose as high as $30 per ton of CO_2, fell to below $10 by mid-2006 and then dropped to near zero in 2007. The EU learned from experience, however, and the second phase, which runs from 2008 to 2012, is expected to be both tougher and more successful. The market has priced these second-phase allowances at $30 to $40 per ton.

Major coal-using countries in the EU face difficult choices in meeting the EU targets. In the United Kingdom, Europe's largest coal importer, the government has been criticized for failing to enunciate a clear policy on coal use, creating uncertainty for proposed new coal-fired power plants. The opposition party recently proposed enacting new emissions standards that would effectively prohibit new coal plants unless they incorporate CCS technology. In Germany, the second-largest importer, new coal-fired capacity is seen as necessary to fill the gap that will result from the planned phaseout of nuclear energy.

The United States has failed to create a national system for reducing greenhouse gas emissions, but there is widespread speculation that a cap-and-trade system will be initiated by 2010. (For a look at how this may evolve, see "How the United States Will Reduce Greenhouse Gases.") Legislative initiatives introduced in the U.S. Congress over the last several years have called for restrictions ranging from merely capping CO_2 emissions at recent levels to reducing them by 90 percent by 2050.

HOW THE UNITED STATES WILL REDUCE GREENHOUSE GASES by T. J. Glauthier

The United States is likely to enact legislation for controlling greenhouse gas emissions in the near future. Over the last two years, we have gotten to the point where the public perception and the perception in Congress are that global warming is a serious problem and that we have to do something about it. The best mechanism for emissions regulation in the United States is a cap-and-trade system with tradable emissions allocations.

One argument in favor of a cap-and-trade system is the political sensitivity to tax increases in the United States. Direct taxation of emissions, which some European countries have adopted, is not an option in this country. These two alternatives, however, are merely different ways of trying to accomplish the same thing.

The tradable emissions allocations that a cap-and-trade system provides are superior to direct taxation in that they give policy makers additional policy levers, such as the ability to phase in requirements in some industries and to set different targets for different sectors. The legislation passed by the U.S. Senate Environment Committee, for example, would allocate allowances to electric utilities, which face the largest costs for complying with emissions reductions, and reduce the allocation over time. The petroleum industry, on the other hand, which supplies the nation's gasoline and diesel fuels, would not be making investments to improve vehicles and therefore would receive no allocations and would start right off paying the full bill.

The implicit price for carbon emissions under a cap-and-trade system will need to be sufficiently high to provide real incentives for emissions reductions.

The level that's being discussed—$30 to $40 per ton—is high enough to affect the kind of power plants that people build. It would increase the costs of operating a typical 500-megawatt coal plant by as much as 70 percent, once it was fully phased in. That cost increase is about the same as the current estimates for adding carbon capture and sequestration technology, so it would provide an incentive to consider that option. Alternatively, companies building new plants might build a natural gas plant, a wind plant, or a nuclear plant instead.

Concerns about a cap-and-trade system for greenhouse gases in the United States include how well it would work, what the compliance costs would be, and what the impact on consumers would be. Looking back at the experience the United States had in the 1990s with reducing the sulfur dioxide emissions that cause acid rain can provide some reassurance. A cap-and-trade system for sulfur dioxide—the first large-scale emissions control system—was set up in 1990, and turned out to be very successful. Emissions were essentially cut in half, compliance costs wound up being only half the amounts originally estimated, and the costs passed along to rate-payers were minimal, increasing their bills by only a few percent. As we look at climate change legislation, we should feel comfortable that we can implement a cap-and-trade system and have it run in a solid, stable way.

The acid rain issue was first raised in the early 1970s, and the nation went through a 20-year period of what I would call socialization as the pros and cons were discussed and legislation was debated, leading to passage of the 1990 acid rain program. In the climate change area, the issue began to be raised around 1988, and the nation has been going through a similar socialization process. Enactment of legislation during the next Congress, 2008–2009, would complete a similar 20-year cycle.

T. J. Glauthier is the chief executive of TJG Energy Associates, LLC, a consulting and executive advisory services company focused on serving clients in the energy sector. Prior to founding TJG Energy Associates, Mr. Glauthier was president and CEO of the Electricity Innovation Institute (an affiliate of the Electric Power Research Institute) from 2001 to 2004, deputy secretary and chief operating officer of the U.S. Department of Energy from 1999 to 2001, and associate director for natural resources, energy and science of the Office of Management and Budget in the White House from 1993 to 1998.

In the United States, an economywide cap-and-trade scheme designed merely to hold greenhouse gas emissions flat would result in a market price of $30 to $40 per ton of CO_2 equivalent. If a system with allowances at those levels is enacted, it will create a strong incentive for coal users to shift to other forms of energy to replace existing coal-fired plants and sharply curtail demand for coal, unless a viable CCS solution is developed. For example, with no limit on greenhouse gas emissions, a Booz & Company analysis estimates that coal demand will rise at an average annual rate of 1.9 percent through 2030; if emissions were held flat, however, demand would fall off at a 2.2 percent annual rate. (See Exhibit 5-5.) This could lead to significantly higher electricity prices in coal-heavy markets. Booz & Company recently conducted a "carbon war game" exercise with seven major investor-owned utilities in the United States. Greenhouse gas restrictions that triggered a transition away from coal-fired generation, the exercise suggested, would drive up real electricity prices by 5 percent per year for a decade. The participants broadly agreed that increases of that magnitude would set off a political firestorm.

Reducing greenhouse gas emissions requires international policy coordination, since individual countries have little incentive to voluntarily reduce their own emissions; indeed, doing so would increase costs and lower the country's competitive advantage. The world began acting collectively to protect the atmosphere in 1997, under the auspices of the United Nations, with the adoption of the Kyoto Protocol, since ratified by 175 countries, which set a collective target of an average 5.2 percent reduction in emissions by 2012. Kyoto's goals were modest, and scientists have criticized the accord, saying that it does too little to slow global warming. The biggest problems with the Kyoto accord, however, are that some nations (most notably the United States, which at the time was the biggest emitter of greenhouse gases) declined to take part, and that many developing nations, including China (which has since passed the United States in greenhouse gas emissions) were excused from meeting specific targets.

Negotiations for the next round of talks to limit greenhouse gases began in late 2007 at a meeting in Bali, where scientists urged the nations in attendance to require mandatory cuts of 50 percent by 2020. The United Nations

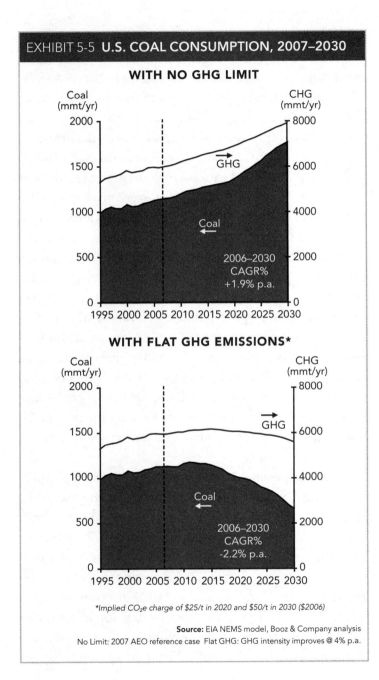

EXHIBIT 5-5 U.S. COAL CONSUMPTION, 2007–2030

WITH NO GHG LIMIT

Coal (mmt/yr) — CHG (mmt/yr)

GHG

Coal

2006–2030
CAGR%
+1.9% p.a.

WITH FLAT GHG EMISSIONS*

Coal (mmt/yr) — CHG (mmt/yr)

GHG

Coal

2006–2030
CAGR%
-2.2% p.a.

*Implied CO_2e charge of $25/t in 2020 and $50/t in 2030 ($2006)

Source: EIA NEMS model, Booz & Company analysis
No Limit: 2007 AEO reference case Flat GHG: GHG intensity improves @ 4% p.a.

recommended that developed nations commit to greenhouse gas reductions of 25 to 40 percent by 2020, and that emerging countries such as China agree to take measurable steps to reduce their emissions. Several nations, however, including the United States and Japan, successfully opposed including numeric targets in the initial proposal.

The most difficult issue that arose at the Bali meeting is that some developed nations, including the United States and Canada, are insisting that the next climate agreement include specific targets for developing nations such as China and India. They note, correctly, that even if the developed nations achieve the suggested reductions in greenhouse gases, increasing emissions from rapidly developing countries could cancel out much of the benefit to the climate. Developing nations argue, also correctly, that the developed nations are responsible for most of the carbon emissions in the atmosphere today, that the per capita emissions of industrialized nations are multiples of those of developing countries, and that a significant percentage of the greenhouse gases in countries like China are emitted in the manufacture of goods that are exported to the industrialized countries.

Solving this standoff will call for all the arts of diplomacy. The developed nations will be asked to make some large concessions to the developing countries before a truly comprehensive agreement can be reached. To allow for their higher per capita usage and their past contributions to global warming, they will be expected to agree to larger reductions in overall emissions than developing countries. It also seems reasonable that developed countries will be expected to subsidize greenhouse gas reductions in the developing world directly. Negotiating such an agreement, and selling it politically in the developed countries, will be enormously difficult, especially given the ongoing financial crisis and the global economic downturn now under way. It is also difficult, however, to envision a new international climate change framework that will be comprehensive enough to make the reductions that scientists deem necessary to slow global warming without some of these elements.

Even if the negotiation of international climate-change agreements is slow and uncertain, there is little doubt that pressure for continued reductions of greenhouse gases will continue in many regions and countries, including the EU and the United States. The pressure to shift away from coal will thus increase as well.

The future of coal is in effect dependent in large part on the legislative plans governments eventually adopt to set the costs of CO_2 emissions, as well as any specific laws directly affecting coal consumption. The other factors affecting coal's fortunes will be the pace of development and commercialization of clean coal technologies and the prices and availability of other fuels. Although renewable energy sources such as wind and solar power may eventually displace coal and other fossil fuels in major applications such as power generation (see Chapter 8), their current share is small and is not expected to grow significantly for a decade or more. For the present, the main alternative to coal is natural gas. As explained in the next chapter, there have been massive upward revisions in estimates of potential gas reserves, largely in the United States and Canada, making it more likely that the power generation industry will favor natural gas as the fuel for future increases in power capacity, at least in the short term.

6

THE PROMISE OF NATURAL GAS

IN A WORLD in which energy prices are rising, concerns about global warming are mounting, and the future of traditional energy sources is increasingly in question, natural gas is the fossil fuel with the best set of attributes. It seems likely to be an important driver of the energy shift, particularly in some regions. Gas is easily substituted for coal in electricity generation, requiring less expensive capital equipment, and there is extensive distribution infrastructure in most developed nations. In addition, natural gas is the most environmentally benign of the fossil fuels, producing fewer harmful by-products than petroleum or coal and only half the greenhouse gases, per unit of energy, of coal. Moreover, natural gas is abundant. One of the most notable recent developments in the world of energy, in fact, is the finding that estimated gas reserves are far higher today than they were just a couple of years ago. Recent technological advances now enable more production from "unconventional" gas reserves that were once uneconomic but can now be extracted cost-effectively at price levels in the range of $5–$7 per thousand cubic feet. Given the new estimates of total reserves and production costs, gas should be sufficient to meet world needs well into the next century. Many of these reserves are in North America (the United States and Canada), which means that natural gas seems likely to play an especially important role in meeting future electricity demand in those countries as the energy shift unfolds.

Historically, natural gas has been the preferred fuel for institutional and industrial heating, as well as for many industrial processes; and since the 1990s, it has also become the preferred fuel for electricity generation. Gas had been gaining market share rapidly in the United States, Europe, and elsewhere during the late 1990s and early 2000s, but then prices roughly doubled. In Europe, this increase was driven by rising oil prices (natural gas and petroleum prices have long been linked there, since the two fuels can be easily substituted in many industrial processes and some generation); in North America, the rise was primarily the result of the dwindling of once plentiful conventional supplies.

The rise in gas prices, however, also had the effect of unlocking reserves of the three different kinds of "unconventional" gas: so-called tight gas, shale gas, and coal bed methane (CBM). These are the same kind of gas as in conventional reserves but are found in geologic formations that make recovery more difficult, requiring special, costly technologies and equipment. At the lower prices that prevailed through the twentieth century, recovering unconventional gas was uneconomic, and as result, it was not counted as part of total reserves. The recent revisions of natural gas reserves that include unconventional reserves have significantly changed the outlook for natural gas, at least in North America. The rise of unconventional gas is recent enough that geologists and information sources like EIA are still busily assessing its impact on global supplies. Some forecasters now estimate that recoverable reserves of unconventional gas in the lower 48 U.S. states, for example, are roughly equal to all proven onshore and offshore reserves of conventional gas, effectively doubling total reserves. These reserves are already being exploited; unconventional gas added nearly 10 percent to U.S. gas production in 2007.

Similarly huge reserves of unconventional gas exist in many other regions and countries. Coal bed methane, for example, is found wherever coal reserves exist; tight gas and shale gas are typically found in the same places as oil and conventional gas. Although commercial extraction is being pursued most actively in the United States, Canada, and Australia, exploration and technical evaluation is under way in more than two dozen countries around the world, including Russia, China, and Indonesia.

RESERVES AND MARKETS

The availability of natural gas is a key indicator to watch for the energy shift. It is also a complex indicator; economies around the world tend to adjust rapidly to the changing realities of natural gas supply. The new supply realities are already having very different effects on various regions. For North America, the effects can be described as potentially transformational: the continent could benefit from self-sufficiency in the most environmentally benign fossil fuel well into the next century, with secure supplies and an extensive installed distribution infrastructure. For other regions, the effects will be varied. In Europe, unconventional gas reserves may also play a part in boosting supplies, but given the relatively low distribution of fossil fuels there and the high level of gas consumption, Europe will remain dependent on imports. Additional supplies of unconventional gas will further boost the reserves and relative resource strength of the existing gas exporters in Russia and other FSU states, as well as in Australia, Africa, and Indonesia.

Unconventional gas supplies will also affect the structure and evolution of the worldwide gas market. Until recently, the future development of natural gas was constrained by supply and distribution issues. The depletion of conventional reserves in Europe and the United States had meant that future demand would have to be supplied increasingly by imports from other regions. This meant either building new pipelines (from the FSU states to Europe and China, for example) or expanding the capacity for liquefied natural gas—the relatively complex and expensive process of liquefying gas by cooling it to minus 260°F, shipping it in specially designed oceangoing tankers (see Exhibit 6-1), and then "regasifying" it for local pipeline delivery and consumption.

There have been additional concerns about the availability, reliability, and security of supplies. Although conventional gas reserves are plentiful, the biggest potential supplies are distant from major consuming markets. Developing the infrastructure both to expand production and

**EXHIBIT 6-1 AN LNG TANKER DOCKING AT AN
OFFSHORE FACILITY IN THE UNITED STATES**

Source: Matt Houston/ Associated Press

to support more LNG capacity is both capital-intensive
and time-consuming. Major gas-producing nations could
opt to use their resources locally, either for electric power
or for industry, rather than selling them for export. Some
producers have shown a recent propensity for "resource
nationalism," calling into question their dependability as
long-term suppliers. Furthermore, many major gas reserves are located primarily in politically unstable regions
(often the same regions that are rich in petroleum), raising concerns about the security of supplies. And finally,
there are concerns that major gas-producing nations may
seek to form a cartel for natural gas, along the lines of
OPEC, to enhance their pricing power.

The markets for natural gas have traditionally been
divided into three largely self-contained regions: the
Americas; Europe, Africa, and the Commonwealth of Independent States (FSU countries); and Asia, Oceania, and

the Middle and Far East. Traditionally, natural gas has been transported via regional and national pipelines. The alternative form of transportation, LNG, involves cooling the substance to a liquid form and carrying it by ship, truck, or rail. This practice, while costly and sometimes difficult, offers far more flexibility than a pipeline, which is fixed in place from source to destination. LNG has been developing since the 1960s, but has begun to reach mass scale only in the last several years. Today, LNG fills about 7 percent of world gas demand and accounts for 22 percent of the international gas trade (with the rest being shipped by pipeline). The International Energy Agency (IEA) expects LNG shipments to grow 6.6 percent per year through 2030, compared with a 2 percent growth rate for natural gas demand, meaning that LNG will account for 50 percent of internationally traded gas in 2030. The market for natural gas seems destined to become more global.

According to recent IEA figures, supply and demand were closely balanced in the three major regions, and interconnectivity through LNG trade was limited. This situation has allowed the emergence and the maintenance of differentiated gas pricing models in each region. In the Americas, prices are determined by short-term contracts indexed to gas market prices, and they generally track with oil prices, since many users can substitute gas and oil for each other. In Europe, prices are mostly determined by long-term contracts based on the "next best alternative" energy source, and they are indexed to commodities like heavy fuel and heating oil prices and, to a lesser extent, coal prices. In the Middle and Far East, prices are based on long-term contracts that are indexed to the "oil product cocktails."

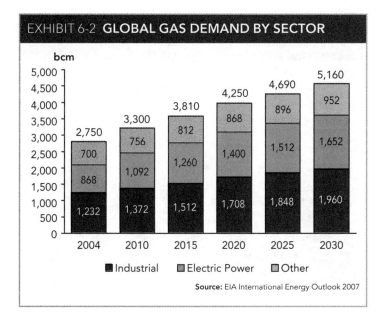

EXHIBIT 6-2 GLOBAL GAS DEMAND BY SECTOR

bcm

Source: EIA International Energy Outlook 2007

The demand for gas is projected to increase robustly. The IEA's *World Energy Outlook* estimates that the cumulative increase in global demand from 2004 to 2030 will be 88 percent (see Exhibit 6-2). The strongest growth will be in the electric power sector (analyzed in Chapter 8); both in oil- and gas-producing nations like Algeria and Libya that are shifting from oil-fired to gas-fired generation and in developed countries, where climate change regulation will provide a strong incentive for shifting from coal to gas. The three traditionally separate regional gas markets will begin to affect one another more strongly as LNG becomes a bigger factor in filling supply shortfalls around the world, but new projections of unconventional gas reserves may have changed that outlook. Previously, it seemed likely that competition for gas in the Atlantic basin would intensify, especially between Europe and the

EXHIBIT 6-3 **CONSTRUCTION OF A GAZPROM PIPELINE TO BRING SIBERIAN GAS TO EUROPE**

Source: Denis Sinyakov/Reuters.

United States. North America's emerging potential in unconventional gas production could make that less likely. It would lower demand for gas imports into the United States, meaning that LNG from the Caribbean, North Africa, and the Middle East would be available to the European market. This, in turn, would improve the continent's fragile gas balance, where security of supplies has been a key concern. Some 40 percent of the EU's gas is imported, and some forecasts envision the percentage rising to as high as 70 percent by 2020. Nearly a third of total gas imports come from Russia (see Exhibit 6-3). The EU has been increasingly concerned about its dependence on imported natural gas since Russia temporarily shut off gas supplies to the Ukraine in 2005. As a result, the EU has moved to build closer relationships with other gas

EXHIBIT 6-4 PROPOSED BROADWATER LNG FACILITY

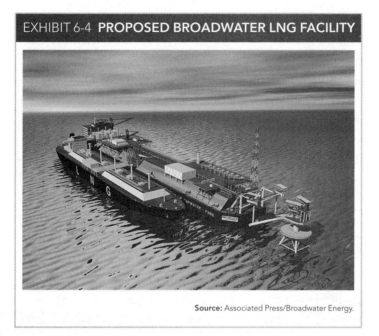

Source: Associated Press/Broadwater Energy.

suppliers—including those in the Middle East, Central Asia, the Caspian and Black Sea area, and Africa—and is looking to increase its usage of LNG.

Use of LNG could vary dramatically among regions. For the United States, LNG will become less important for meeting demand growth as North American unconventional reserves are developed. LNG accounts for only 3 percent of U.S. consumption today. For Europe, the growth in the LNG market will mean greater diversity and availability of gas supplies; some forecasts suggest that LNG could supply 25 percent of European demand in the long term.

In the near to intermediate term, the growth of LNG is not likely to be constrained by the number of regasification terminals in either region. There are currently 14 LNG terminals in Europe, 6 more under construction, and plans for more than 25 others. In the United States, there are 5 terminals in operation and 3 under construction. And although there have been plans for more than 20 others, potential future supplies of unconventional domestic gas will make them less necessary. Construction of LNG terminals, in general, may be constrained by "not in my backyard (NIMBY)" opposition. This has been true especially in the United States, where some planned sites (such as the Broadwater terminal, planned for Long Island Sound near New York, shown in Exhibit 6-4) have been blocked for years, as well as by the increasing costs and longer lead times that have recently been affecting large energy infrastructure projects of all kinds.

Looking farther ahead, the implications of increased demand for gas as a result of CO_2 regulation are difficult to predict. Nuclear capacity could come on stream at some point in the future, as could low-CO_2 coal-fired capacity, reducing the need for natural gas. The expanded supply outlook for gas, however, may keep future prices low enough to obviate the need for these alternatives. On the other hand, if the transportation sector shifts toward electricity as a fuel source over the long term, one result could be a substantial addition to base load power demand, increasing the need for larger gas supplies. If more extensive LNG infrastructure should be necessary in the future, offshore regasification facilities could be built to increase capacity. This relatively new technology is significantly less capital-intensive than land-based facilities, faces fewer licensing hurdles, has relatively short lead times to operation, and, importantly, is flexible and can be moved elsewhere when demand patterns shift.

SUPPLY-SIDE UNCERTAINTIES

Gas-importing regions will continue to face a major concern about the speed with which known gas reserves will
be developed into production, and whether the gas will be
available on the world market. One set of challenges lies in
developing these reserves given the current constraints on
the availability of equipment, capital, and engineers and
other human resources for major infrastructure projects.
Indeed, these are exactly the same resources that the oil
industry is competing for, and the human resource challenge is widely recognized as one of the threats to the growth
of the oil and gas business.

In addition, the recent economic boom in the Middle
East may lead to an explosive increase in local demand, especially in gas-to-power, thereby reducing the possibility
of making more LNG available for exports at least in the
short to mid-term. Other options for gas producers include building gas-to-liquids plants, developing chemi-
cal and fertilizer production, or simply injecting the gas
into oil wells to boost oil production. In a world in which
labor and resources for capital projects are in short supply, it's not obvious that making gas available through LNG
makes the most sense for some producers.

There are also uncertainties about future infrastructure additions as a result of geopolitical instability. Gas
infrastructure additions require huge investments and
typically have very long lead times. Geopolitical and strategic considerations by market participants can introduce
possible delays in construction or even doubts about the
credibility of announced pipeline projects. Examples are

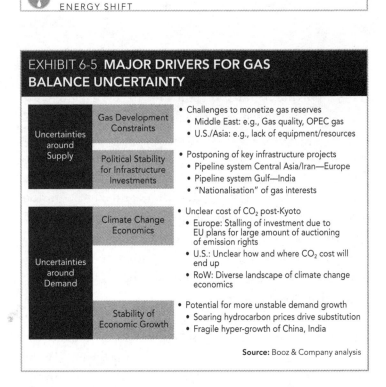

EXHIBIT 6-5 MAJOR DRIVERS FOR GAS BALANCE UNCERTAINTY

Uncertainties around Supply	Gas Development Constraints	• Challenges to monetize gas reserves • Middle East: e.g., Gas quality, OPEC gas • U.S./Asia: e.g., lack of equipment/resources
	Political Stability for Infrastructure Investments	• Postponing of key infrastructure projects • Pipeline system Central Asia/Iran—Europe • Pipeline system Gulf—India • "Nationalisation" of gas interests
Uncertainties around Demand	Climate Change Economics	• Unclear cost of CO_2 post-Kyoto • Europe: Stalling of investment due to EU plans for large amount of auctioning of emission rights • U.S.: Unclear how and where CO_2 cost will end up • RoW: Diverse landscape of climate change economics
	Stability of Economic Growth	• Potential for more unstable demand growth • Soaring hydrocarbon prices drive substitution • Fragile hyper-growth of China, India

Source: Booz & Company analysis

the Nabucco pipeline, proposed to transport gas from the Caspian region via Turkey to Austria via Bulgaria, Romania, and Hungary, and the projected pipeline linking the Gulf region with India. Furthermore, efforts to nationalize gas assets (and other natural resources) can present specific challenges to investors, such as the developments involving a number of Western oil and gas majors in Russia (see Exhibit 6-5).

The Middle East lies at the center of market uncertainties, both as a producer and, to an increasing extent, as a consumer. Yet it will continue to play a key role in global gas markets because of the fact that the Middle East currently accounts for some two-fifths of the world's proven gas reserves. With over 28 trillion cubic meters (tcm), or some 15.5 percent of the global total, Iran has the region's largest known conventional gas reserves, followed by Qatar with 25.4 tcm, or 14 percent of the global total.

The IEA's base-case forecast is that the region's gas demand will grow at roughly 4.2 percent per annum until 2015, driven by steep growth in gas-fueled power generation, leaving some 189 billion cubic meters (bcm) available for export by 2015. Thereafter, overall annual demand growth is expected to ease to 3.6 percent, despite the continued strong growth in gas-to-power, leaving some 232 bcm available for export by 2030.

But what would happen if a number of key Middle Eastern countries cannot deliver such incremental exports? Reasons could include increased use of gas for reinjection for oil recovery, production constraints on oil-associated gas as a result of OPEC oil quotas, continued geopolitical instability, or increasing gas consumption within the region. The recent economic boom is leading to a surge in domestic gas demand not only for power generation but also for higher value-added industrial uses, such as petrochemicals and fertilizers. Low prices have made gas the primary fuel for regional economic growth.

According to a Booz & Company analysis, world markets should be able to adjust without too much difficulty if Middle East gas exports turn out to be significantly less than assumed in the base case. Lower growth in exports to Europe from Oman and Qatar would be replaced by Nigerian LNG, and the balance in the Asian gas market could be maintained by increased expected supplies from Australia and Sakhalin. The prevalent gas price regimes would be largely unaffected.

AN "OGEC" IN THE MAKING?

Gas producers outside the Middle East should have opportunities to exploit what are likely to be significant medium-term export growth opportunities. Uncertainty associated with CO_2 targets and gas development constraints should improve the market position of Russian and African gas producers in particular, but long-term gas demand uncertainties create a high risk of overinvestment in infrastructure. Major suppliers, such as Russia, will thus need to build a network of commercial links to other gas producers to prepare for swings in gas demand. This could lead to the emergence of a de facto OPEC for gas—sometimes envisioned as an Organization of Gas Exporting Countries (OGEC). Another factor arguing in favor of the emergence of such a cartel is the upward revision in estimates of world gas reserves from unconventional gas. As real and potential supplies increase, pressure will build for lower prices in the future. A smoothly functioning OGEC could help major gas producers coordinate their production to maximize their pricing power.

Russia's Gazprom—which holds 30 to 40 percent of the world's conventional gas reserves—has been increasingly active recently in forging links with other gas suppliers. It has signed a memorandum of understanding with Algeria's state-owned Sonatrach consortium, paving the way for greater cooperation in the field of gas exploration, extraction, and supply. It has begun negotiations with the Nigerian government to invest $2.5 billion in gas projects, in exchange for access to gas fields or LNG. Gazprom is one of the companies that are short-listed to explore offshore blocks in Libya.

The increased activity of non-Middle East gas producers poses a challenge for the major gas producers in the
Middle East. Since Nigeria and Russia are poised to become incremental suppliers to more markets, Middle East
gas producers need, as a matter of some urgency, to for-
mulate a view of their incremental export potential and
decide whether, given demand uncertainty, it makes sense
to export more gas. If it does make sense, they need to develop a plan for increasing their exports before Nigeria and
Russia act. On the supply side, sustained high gas prices
are making new techniques for developing deepwater offshore and sour gas reserves interesting investment opportunities. On the demand side, Middle East gas producers
should intensify their efforts to improve the efficiency of
their domestic energy use.

DECODING THE FUTURE OF GAS

The rise of unconventional gas supplies and the development of greater connectivity between the world's natural
gas markets will determine the longer-term outlook for
gas's future as an energy source. That future looks much
brighter today than it did just a few years ago. In North
America, unconventional supplies will make gas a more
obvious choice for meeting future demand for electricity.
If tough U.S. greenhouse gas regulations are enacted, it will
mean even faster growth in gas-to-power. Imports will become less necessary, obviating the need for further LNG
development, and the outlook for other fuels, notably coal
and nuclear, will darken. Europe will be in much the same
position as in the past, and EU efforts to diversify gas

supplies will favor LNG investment. Outside North America, the gas markets will likely become increasingly global.

Many of the answers to the questions about the future of the natural gas market will depend on the future path of prices as unconventional gas suppliers are developed. If supplies expand as greatly as many predict, future gas prices should rise less quickly than prices for other fuels, increasing the overall attractiveness of gas as an energy source, with major implications for electric power generation, the subject of Chapter 8. The main potential negatives for the future of gas are the possible formulation of a gas producers' cartel and the possibility of political instability that would call into question supplies from major gas producers.

7

THE UNCERTAIN PATH TO CLEAN ENERGY

LOOKING BEYOND the intermediate term, there are two nonfossil options for meeting a major share of future electricity demand in a carbon-constrained world: nuclear energy and renewables. Both have tremendous promise; neither, however, is well-positioned today to be the "silver bullet" that will supply abundant amounts of carbon-free energy to meet future world demand. Nuclear energy already plays a significant role in electricity generation, but there are long lead times in building nuclear plants, deep uncertainties about the ultimate costs, and lingering questions about safety and security of nuclear waste. Renewables, including wind, solar and biomass, are the fastest growing energy source, but they are starting from a very small base, are still maturing technologically, and in most cases need governmental support to compete with other fuels on price. No significant increase in nuclear-generating capacity is likely before 2018 in most nations, and the long-term outlook is unclear. Renewables, given the current trend lines, seem unlikely to play a large role in the energy shift between now and 2030. What would be needed for either of these carbon-free alternative energy sources to grow quickly enough to make significant inroads into fossil fuels' share of electricity generation is a big, sustained push from governments.

NUCLEAR POWER

Like renewable energy sources, nuclear energy produces no greenhouse gases in operation. Unlike renewables (other than hydroelectric power), nuclear power already commands a significant market share—15 percent of total world power generation, surpassed by only coal and natural gas. There are currently 439 nuclear plants operating in 31 countries. Building large numbers of additional nuclear plants could meet a far greater proportion of the world's future energy needs using current technology, and thus could be a major mitigating factor in greenhouse gas emissions. Plans are under way to significantly increase the number of nuclear plants around the world. China has the most ambitious nuclear program, with 31 reactors under construction or planned, followed by Russia, Japan, and India. In the United States, 7 plants are in the formal planning stages, and proposals have been made to build 25 more.

The nuclear power industry, however, faces significant challenges and uncertainties in building future capacity in many countries, including persistent fears about safety and a long record of cost overruns, construction delays, and regulatory red tape. Concerns remain about the disposal of nuclear waste and the dangers of waste being converted into nuclear weapons, leading to further weapons proliferation and geopolitical instability. Nuclear plants are also expensive: a single plant can cost as much as $9 billion, including financing. One constraint on the future of nuclear power development is uncertainty about its costs. In the past, most nuclear plants have wound up costing two to three times more than their original estimates, and long delays have been the rule rather than the exception. Some of the projects under way, such as a new reactor at Finland's Olkiluoto plant, are already far over budget and behind schedule.

Another constraint is the limited number of trained engineers, skilled craft laborers, and other personnel, and the tight supply chain for nuclear power components. During the decades in which little new nuclear capacity was being built, many component manufacturers abandoned the business. Only one steel company, for example (Japan Steel Works), is currently making the large containment vessels (the size of a six-story building) that nuclear plants require.

All told, there are proposals at various stages for more than 200 new nuclear plants around the world. But the earliest that most of them will come on line is around 2018, and the supply-chain problems suggest that future growth in the industry may be slow, except, possibly, in China. While new nuclear plants will help supply growing energy needs, particularly in the developing world, most industry experts think that their numbers will be insufficient to displace the need for new additional capacity from other energy sources in the next two to three decades. (See "Nuclear Power in the Developed and Developing World.")

NUCLEAR POWER IN THE DEVELOPED AND DEVELOPING WORLD by Joan MacNaughton

We are likely to see modest increases in nuclear energy capacity in countries with highly developed economies, such as the United Kingdom, and a great deal of activity in the newly industrializing economies. Attitudes about nuclear energy in the United Kingdom have changed markedly in the past few years, driven by concerns about both energy security and climate change. One event that affected people's consciousness in a big way was the dispute between Russia and the Ukraine over natural gas supplies in 2006, and the similar dispute between Russia and Belarus over oil a year later. Another was a very big spike in gas prices in the winter of 2005–2006, which resulted from several different circumstances coming together. People began to feel that they didn't want to be as dependent on gas as they would be if we didn't have nuclear energy, and that perhaps nuclear energy should be an important contributor to the energy mix. At the same time, the profile of climate change, and people's concern about it, was increasing hugely.

Up until last year, the government's attitude toward nuclear energy had been lukewarm for several years: it hadn't ruled nuclear energy out, but it hadn't positively encouraged it. The government had been encouraging renewable energy sources, but renewables were penetrating the energy mix at quite a low rate. People began to think that maybe renewables, on their own, weren't the whole answer.

As for the outlook for new nuclear capacity, policy makers in the United Kingdom are not likely to set a precise target for future nuclear capacity. We don't have a system where the government or policy makers, by and large, prescribe how large a share one form of energy should have relative to another, although there is a specific target for renewables. Obviously, we will have to build quite a number of power stations to replace those that have recently been retired or are expected to be retired over the next 10 to 20 years. So you might think of nuclear maintaining its share of the current energy mix. Given the time scales involved, that may be as ambitious as the marketplace is likely to be. But, having said that, a combination of a high carbon price and high prices for fossil fuels might drive a bigger investment program.

The newly industrializing countries, on the other hand, are likely to move very fast on nuclear. Many of them have a significant mismatch between the amount of electricity generation that their economies now require and what they are currently able to provide. Given the trend in oil and gas prices over the last few years, and the expected trend over the next

10 years, I would be amazed if those countries did not see nuclear as a very competitive option. Many of them do not have the same constraints on building nuclear plants that countries with highly developed economies have, so they have the ability to build quickly. I suspect that they also see nuclear energy as a way of showing that they are economically advanced; there's a kind of cachet to being able to have nuclear energy.

There are concerns about nuclear waste, but there is already a lot of it around—some of it in places where the security and control regimes may not be the most up-to-date. I don't think there's much sense in trying to deny newly industrializing economies access to the kind of power that other countries already have, nor would it be right. Instead, we should focus on making sure that new projects comply with best practices in the control of material and record keeping. At the same time, we should press on with the good work that is going on to bring some of the legacy sites up to best practices.

Given the hiatus that we've had in building new nuclear plants, there is a shortage of people in the field who are qualified and experienced. Many people have left the sector, and those who remain are from older generations and are near retirement. A big effort should be made to keep them around as long as possible to exploit their knowledge and skills, and to see that their knowledge and skills are transferred to younger members of the workforce.

Most important, there needs to be a very clear signal that nuclear energy is going to be a great industry and that it is going to be around for many years. If that happens, businesses will gear up and invest in both people and projects. But there needs to be confidence that it is going to happen, that it will happen on a reasonable time scale, and that it is going to be a sustained area of activity.

Joan MacNaughton is senior vice president, power and environment policies, ALSTOM Power Systems. She is a former civil servant, having been principal private secretary to the deputy prime minister and two home secretaries. Ms. MacNaughton was director general energy (and then director general international energy security) at the U.K. Department of Trade and Industry from 2002 to 2007. In this position, she led on the energy aspects of the Gleneagles G8 Programme of Action and on the energy agenda during the U.K.'s presidency of the EU. She was chairman of the International Energy Agency.

Putting nuclear energy on the kind of aggressive growth path that could drive the energy shift in the decades ahead seems unlikely without large-scale government support. Few private sector companies can be expected to make the kinds of multi-billion-dollar long-term bets that nuclear-plant construction requires, given the uncertainties about construction costs, waste storage, and future regulatory regimes. Moreover, government support would need to be both long-term and credible. The past experience of the power generation industry with government regulation of nuclear power, covered in the next chapter, is not likely to inspire confidence about the future. The most likely path for nuclear energy today seems to be for modest increases in capacity, which should roughly maintain its current market share among fuels for stationary applications.

WIND, SOLAR, AND OTHER RENEWABLES

Renewable energy sources present a very different set of challenges from nuclear energy. While their market share is very small today, they hold tremendous promise for meeting the world's future need for electricity. And given the realities of global warming and the increasing pressure from policy makers and public opinion, renewables are likely to be the fastest-growing source of energy in the next decades.

Indeed, many governmental entities, from the supranational to the national, state or provincial, and municipal level, have announced goals or targets for increasing the percentage of renewables in total energy consumption. The most comprehensive such initiative is the EU's binding target, approved by its 27 member nations, to supply 20 percent of total energy needs from renewable sources by 2020, up from 6.5 percent today. In addition, more than 20 other countries, including 13 developing countries, have set targets for renewables, as have many states, provinces, and municipalities in the United States and Canada. Some 56 countries have renewable energy promotion policies, and more than 35 have adopted feed-in tariffs for renewable electricity (these require public utilities to buy electricity generated by renewables at above-market rates, with the additional costs spread over the utilities' customer bases.)

Wind power is currently the most technologically mature and scalable renewable energy source, and the best positioned to gain market share against other energy sources. The number of wind power installations around the world has increased dramatically over the past decade. The current technology is dependable, and the costs of wind development sited onshore are approaching parity with those of traditional fossil fuel generation when subsidies are included, as a result of advances in efficiency and unit-cost reductions as scale has increased. Today, wind is at parity without subsidies when natural gas prices hit about $8 per thousand cubic feet, and it can be highly profitable when subsidies are factored in. Wind power is carbon-free in operation. Its chief disadvantage is that wind is intermittent in most places, making it an unsuitable source for providing base load energy during periods of peak demand. As a result, substantial deployment of wind energy for power generation would require either substantial back-up power from other energy sources or large amounts of electricity storage capacity. Several technologies have been suggested for this purpose, but they are either in the R&D stage or have not been tested at commercial levels of operation. Another disadvantage is that many of the best locations for wind power are not near major population centers and therefore will require significant infrastructure development of the transmission grid. Several countries, however, are now demonstrating that their power grids can operate with significant portions of their energy supplied by wind. Denmark, for example, has

EXHIBIT 7-1 **VESTAS WIND TURBINE COMPONENTS IN DENMARK**

Source: Sigrid Nygaard/AFP/Getty Images.

been a leader in wind technology (see Exhibit 7-1), and currently derives 20 percent of its electricity from wind. Future advances in storage technology could allow even higher percentages.

One factor holding back faster growth in wind power has been a supply-chain bottleneck in wind turbine production. Another is the difficulty of situating new facilities for NIMBY reasons. Many people find wind farms aesthetically unattractive. The next frontier for increasing wind production is the mass development of offshore wind farms, located out of sight of land. Only five nations have operating offshore wind farms today: Denmark, Sweden, the United Kingdom, the Netherlands, and Ireland (see Exhibit 7-2).

EXHIBIT 7-2 AN OFFSHORE WIND FARM UNDER CONSTRUCTION OFF THE COAST OF THE NETHERLANDS

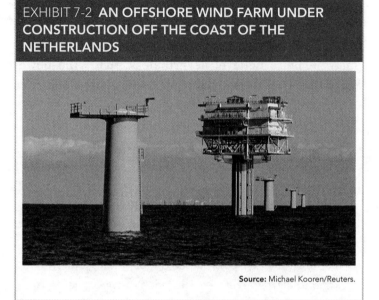

Source: Michael Kooren/Reuters.

The European Wind Energy Association estimates that offshore wind could supply 4 percent of Europe's power consumption by 2020, and ultimately could be deployed on a much wider scale. Developing 5 percent of the North Sea's surface area, the association says, could supply about 25 percent of Europe's future electricity needs. In the United States, a recent report by the Department of Energy (DOE) concluded that it would be feasible to build enough wind capacity to supply 20 percent of U.S. electricity needs by 2020, but only if capital costs of wind power fall significantly, efficiency improves, and energy consumers absorb half the costs. The footprint of land-based wind turbines and related facilities under this scenario could require nearly 1,000 square miles of land—nearly the size of the state of Rhode Island. In addition, the DOE esti-mates that some 12,650 miles of new transmission lines would need to be built, at a cost of $60 billion. Some in-dustry experts believe, nevertheless, that wind power could supply 10 percent of world energy by 2020. (See "The Potential for Wind Power.")

THE POTENTIAL FOR WIND POWER by Ditlev Engel

Wind power is a clean and independent energy source that can be installed very quickly and that meets today's policy needs for enhancing energy security, reducing dependence on fossil fuels, and mitigating climate change. The price of wind energy is both predictable and competitive, and the technology is extremely dependable. In the past, wind was seen simply as an alternative form of energy; today, it is a large-scale, reliable source of energy that has been integrated into the energy mix along with oil and gas. In comparison with other renewable sources, wind energy is *the* most mature and competitive technology.

Europe is currently the biggest market for wind energy, with almost two-thirds of the world's cumulative capacity. However, other regions, like the United States and Asia, are catching up very quickly.

The North American market has experienced the largest growth worldwide during the past two years. The Global Wind Energy Council predicted in 2006 that the United States would be the most important global market for wind power during the period 2007–2010, with an average growth of 3,500 megawatts of new capacity per year. The United States is expected to overtake Germany as the largest market for wind energy by the end of 2009, provided that growth continues at the current rate.

Growth in the Asian markets has also been breathtaking: In 2007, over a quarter of all new worldwide capacity was installed on the Asian continent. In China, the growth rate and the number of total installations more than doubled in 2007 compared to 2006.

One of the main drivers for the global wind energy buildup is the strong political focus on reducing CO_2 emissions to combat climate change. The Kyoto Protocol and the EU climate plan are two major political initiatives. The establishment of a high and stable price for carbon globally will favor those technologies that deliver carbon-neutral energy, such as wind energy. Moreover, the global discussions taking place at international policy meetings, such as the Conferences of UN Parties, the G8, and the World Economic Forum summit, are also significant drivers of the macromarket.

However, the carbon market and climate policies are still very far from being genuine direct market drivers for wind energy. For many years to come, the most important factor leading the change will continue to be national policies that support renewable energy sources. This can be seen clearly in the outline of the recent EU 2020 renewable energy directive proposal, which emphasizes the need for action at the national level. Such action will be especially important in the critical period between now and 2020, when greenhouse gas emissions must peak and begin to decline if we are to avoid the worst impacts of climate change.

Another advantage of wind power is that it has the smallest water consumption per unit of energy produced of any kind of energy generation: wind turbines do not use any water at all when generating electricity. A recent Intergovernmental Panel on Climate Change report concluded that some of the major challenges of global warming will be related to water-resource development and management.

By 2030, most of the existing power-generation capacity will have to be renewed. Taking into account the clear advantages of wind energy over conventional fossil fuels and other renewables, Vestas believes that there is vast wind energy market potential to be exploited, and sound reasons to believe that wind power will be integrated into most countries' energy-generation mix on a par with other traditional energy technologies.

Vestas's goal is to have at least 10 percent of the world's power production based on wind energy by 2020. To achieve this, the wind turbine industry must install a total of around 1 million megawatts over the next 13 years. Today, the global share of wind energy is less than 1 percent of the worldwide electricity demand. If the goal of 10 percent is reached, wind power as a single energy source will account for 15 percent of the CO_2 reduction requirement for 2020 set forth by the United Nations Framework Convention on Climate Change.

Ditlev Engel is president and chief executive officer of Vestas, which leads the wind energy market with a 28 percent share. Vestas has installed over 33,500 wind turbines in 63 countries on five continents. During the last 25 years, the capacity of Vestas wind turbines has grown 100fold, from 30 kilowatts to 3 megawatts. In total, Vestas turbines today generate more than 50 million megawatts a year, enough power to provide electricity for every household in a country the size of Spain, with its population of more than 40 million.

Wind power is thus the best developed renewable technology for generating electricity, but significant hurdles—including land use, storage, and transmission—would need to be overcome before it could grow to the point where it would make double-digit market share inroads into world energy demand. Given the current economics, wind power will also require significant, sustained governmental support. Wind power seems likely, therefore, to be an important component in the energy shift, but it will not, by itself, be a solution to the challenge of meeting future world energy demand.

Related technologies to harness wave and tidal power are in their infancy, although several nations—notably the United Kingdom—are encouraging further development.

Solar energy is the next most promising renewable technology. Like wind, solar power is intermittent, but its advantage is that it generates most of its electricity on warm, sunny days, when electric power use is at its highest in many markets. Solar power also produces no greenhouse gases. It faces some of the same challenges as wind power, including the need for storage and transmission.

There are two major types of solar power generation. The first and most familiar is photovoltaic, which uses silicon-based solar panels to convert sunlight to electricity. These panels are often arrayed on the roofs of houses and commercial buildings. Solar panels, popular with environmentally minded homeowners and businesses, are subsidized by governments in many places. In China, solar panels are used on a mass scale for water heating; they provide hot water for some 30 million homes.

Using photovoltaic solar technology to generate electric power is not currently cost-competitive with the use of fossil fuels without subsidies, but several countries, led by Germany, Japan, and Spain, have built sizable photovoltaic solar power plants. Growth in photovoltaic solar power has been constrained by a shortage of manufacturing capacity for the silicon used to make solar cells. However, more than a dozen companies in Europe, China, Japan, and the United States are investing in new manufacturing capacity, and the industry is predicting significant reductions in costs that could accelerate commercialization. Overall, it seems likely that the total costs of photovoltaic generation will drop by about 50 percent by 2020, at which point photovoltaic generation will reach "grid parity"—where it could compete with conventional generation sources without subsidies—in some countries and regions.

The second type, thermal solar, is not experiencing as rapid a drop in costs, but it could become more competitive as new generations of plants are built. Thermal solar (also called concentrated solar) plants use arrays of mirrors to concentrate sunlight on water-filled tubes, producing steam to drive turbines that generate electricity. The plants can also store heat as highly pressurized steam (or, under one new technology, as molten salt), allowing them to produce electricity at night as well as in the daytime. Several plants using early versions of the technology were built in the Mojave Desert in the United States in the late 1980s, including Solar Energy Generating Systems, a nine-plant unit owned by FPL Energy. It uses 1 million mirrors covering 1,600 acres to produce 354 megawatts (about two-thirds the size of a typical coal-fired plant) and is the world's largest solar plant.

Over the last few years, significant investment has flowed into thermal solar. Demonstration projects have been built in Europe, and the first of three small thermal-solar power plants began operating in Spain in 2006 (see Exhibit 7-3). Some 5.8 gigawatts of solar thermal capacity was in planning stages around the world in late 2007, including plants designed to produce as much power as conventional fossil fuel plants. If these plants live up to expectations and can produce electricity at costs near those of fossil fuel plants, the technology could change the face of electric power in the coming decades. Ausla, a Silicon Valley startup that plans to build 1 gigawatt worth of thermal solar capacity in the United States over the next seven years, boasts that using its current technologies, "all U.S. electric power, day and night, can be generated using a land area of roughly 8,500 square miles."

Solar power is thus highly promising in the long term, particularly since the chief obstacles to its wider adoption

EXHIBIT 7-3 **THERMAL SOLAR PLANT NEAR SEVILLE, SPAIN**

Source: Javier Barbancho/Reuters.

are technological, and therefore amenable to solutions from science and business innovation. But in terms of world energy use, solar is starting from a base of nearly zero, so even if technological progress is rapid, and new solar capacity were to be built on a massive scale, it would have a minimal effect on the mix of world energy uses over the next decade or more.

The next most promising renewable energy source, biomass energy—power derived from burning forestry, agricultural, and municipal waste, and from methane gas collected in landfills—is another small part of world supply, though it has been, historically, the largest nonhydro renewable in the developing world, North America, and in the Nordic countries of Europe. Biomass is a carbon-free energy source, since the CO_2 that is released during its combustion was previously captured by the plants used as feedstocks. Biomass is an important component of the EU's plans for increasing renewables' share of total energy.

Biomass is used to power small electricity plants and in combined heat and power (CHP) plants, and is also used to co-fire coal plants. Finland is the leader in electricity generation from biomass, deriving 12 percent of its total electricity generation from bioenergy, mostly from forestry by-products. Other nations that are leading in this area include Sweden, Denmark, and Germany. Worldwide, biomass accounts for about 1 percent of electricity generation, but capacity has been growing at double-digit rates in many countries. According to a 2005 EU report, the most effective subsidies for biomass have been Denmark's feed-in tariffs and Finland's tax-relief program. The EU found that half its member countries need to provide further support to increase biomass power generation.

Geothermal energy, which taps into underground sources of steam, produces no greenhouse gases, but it is practical only in particular geological situations. The United States is the largest producer, with plants concentrated in five Western states producing about 3 gigawatts of electricity. Some studies have estimated that significant increases are feasible, but the science and technology for finding and exploiting geothermal energy are not well developed. Iceland, with a high concentration of volcanoes, produces 26 percent of its electricity and 87 percent of home heating from geothermal energy.

Hydroelectric power is the only renewable energy source that supplies a significant share of electricity demand today; at 16 percent it is roughly equal to nuclear power. Hydro is carbon free, promotes energy security, and has low operating costs, but future growth is limited. Most of the choicest sites have already been developed in industrialized countries, and both environmental and local opposition to large hydro projects has slowed their growth. Most future capacity is expected to be added in developing nations in Asia and Africa. Environmental concerns may prove to be the biggest constraint on future growth and are slowing projects even in China, which has developed more hydro capacity than any other nation in recent decades. Hydro's current 16 percent share of total electricity generation is down from 21.5 percent in 1973, and is expected to continue to decline.

THE CASE FOR CARBON-FREE ENERGY

Nonfossil alternative fuels will become increasingly important as the world shifts to a lower-carbon future. Nuclear energy, with its current significant share in power-generation supply, remains essential for meeting greenhouse gas emissions targets, and continued increases in nuclear capacity are likely, although many of the new plants now under way will likely be offset by phase-outs of older plants. But as we'll see in the discussion of power generation in the next chapter, nuclear power will be subject to stiff cost competition in the short term from natural gas, and from continued policy competition from renewable energy sources such as wind and solar power in the longer term.

Wind and solar power (and to a lesser extent, biomass) are the renewable energy sources with the most promising long-term outlook, but they face significant hurdles to large-scale growth and seem unlikely to achieve large market shares in the next two decades based on their current growth rate and outlook. In order for them to play a larger role in the energy shift, fossil fuel prices would need to remain at very high levels, and stringent greenhouse gas regulations would have to be imposed on fossil fuels. Significant technological breakthroughs would be required, and governments would need to continue support through aggressive subsidies, while making a credible case that their commitment was long-term.

THE POWER-
GENERATION
PUZZLE

MEETING THE WORLD'S growing demand
for electric power while limiting the emission of greenhouse
gases is the most urgent imperative for energy policy in the
twenty-first century. It will also present some of the most
complex, costly, and risky business challenges that energy
companies and governments have ever faced. The combustion of fossil fuels—especially coal—to generate electricity
today is responsible for more greenhouse gas emissions
than industry and all forms of transport combined. The investments that will be required to build new power generation capacity over the next few decades will be measured
in trillions of dollars, and the risks and uncertainties involved in choosing among the range of fuel sources are vast.

The need for increased capacity will be relentless. Demand for electricity has closely tracked growth in GDP since

World War II, and given standard forecasts of economic growth, electricity consumption is likely to double by 2030. Demand will rise steadily in the developed nations, but far faster in the developing world. (See Exhibit 8-1.) North America and the European Union together will account for 21 percent of the growth in electricity generation through 2030; China and India will account for 43 percent. Unless the mix of fuels changes dramatically, greenhouse gas emission will rise to unacceptable levels: In "business as usual" projections, CO_2 emissions from the power sector will increase by two-thirds over the same period, making power generation the fastest-growing cause of climate change.

One apparent option for mitigating this effect would be to reduce the growth of electricity demand by encouraging conservation. Attractive as this may seem, however, the close connection between electricity demand and GDP growth suggests that it is unrealistic to expect a large effect. An increased emphasis on conservation could slow demand growth significantly in mature, industrialized economies, as could rising electricity prices. Demand could also be constrained sharply in the medium term if governments were to allow higher energy prices to flow directly into higher consumer electricity prices by eliminating subsidies and regulatory roadblocks. Such moves, however, are politically painful. As noted in Chapter 2, the best historical evidence for the efficacy of conservation is found in the reaction to the energy crises of the 1970s, when some European nations, and also U.S. states like California, adopted conservation policies. But most of the increases in world GDP over the next decades will happen in newly industrializing nations, where conservation is likely to take a back seat to economic development. One

EXHIBIT 8-1 ELECTRICITY DEMAND AGAINST GDP PER CAPITA

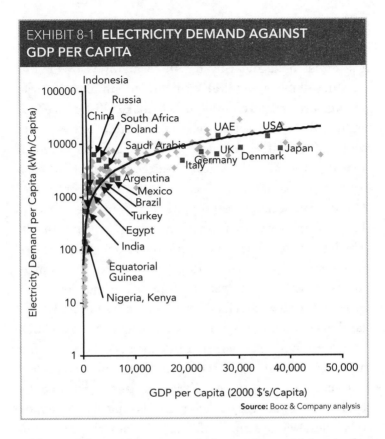

Source: Booz & Company analysis

additional factor that may push demand even higher in the future is the advent of electricity as an alternative energy source for transportation: to the extent that plug-in hybrids and all-electric vehicles succeed in the marketplace, they will increase the demand for electricity in proportion to the decrease in demand for petroleum that they create.

Among the leading myths about energy today is that renewable, environmentally friendly energy sources such as wind and solar energy will be able to supply future needs for power generation easily. A look at the energy sources that currently supply world energy production shows why the mix of fuels used for electricity generation today is incompatible with policies designed to reduce greenhouse gas emissions, and why it will be many years—if not decades—before renewables begin to supplant a large enough proportion of fossil fuels to make a difference (see Exhibit 8-2). Coal is the leading fuel source for electricity generation, with a 40 percent share, and, as noted in Chapter 5, is also the leading source of greenhouse gas emissions. Natural gas is second, with a 20 percent share. Oil-fired generation still supplies 6 percent of electricity, but its share has been decreasing and will continue to fall. The leading nonfossil energy source for electricity is hydroelectric power, with a 16 percent share. Hydro produces no greenhouse gases in operation, but its future growth is limited, and it presents other environmental and land-use concerns. Next comes nuclear energy, which makes up another 15 percent of electricity generation. But although nuclear power is carbon-free, it presents safety and security concerns, as well as investment risk, and the lead time for building nuclear plants is long in many countries. Renewable sources of energy for power generation, including wind, solar, geothermal, biomass, and waste together, account for less than 3 percent of total world power generation.

As Exhibit 8-2 shows, the baseline projections of the IEA, based on current trends and policies, don't show much change in the mix of fuels for electricity generation from now to 2030. While the share of renewables grows rapidly in percentage terms, the absolute growth of coal is quite large. Thus, any realistic plan to limit or reduce greenhouse gas emissions and slow global warming over the next few decades will need to bring about a huge shift in this mix.

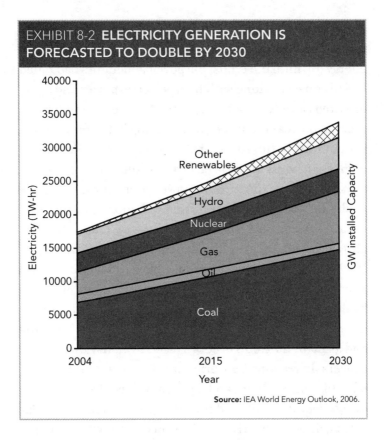

EXHIBIT 8-2 **ELECTRICITY GENERATION IS FORECASTED TO DOUBLE BY 2030**

Source: IEA World Energy Outlook, 2006.

BIG BETS, PAST AND PRESENT

The situation today as companies and nations try to plan for future demand in a carbon-constrained world is one of turmoil, because of the many different options among technologies and fuels—and the turmoil is likely to continue for a long time.

Historically, the world has swung wildly between different approaches to electricity generation, and the electricity sector has gone through two major building cycles with different fuels over the last four decades. The first was nuclear energy. Up until the 1960s, the power generators had relied heavily on coal, along with hydroelectric power and some oil-fired capacity in some regions. But when the first commercial nuclear plants began operating in the mid-1950s, proponents believed that nuclear power could generate endless amounts of cheap electricity. Nuclear capacity rose steadily through the 1970s as power companies, especially in the United States, committed to major building programs. Safety concerns mounted, however, after the nuclear accident at Three Mile Island in the United States in 1979 (even though the accident caused no fatalities, and later studies found that there were practically no detectable health effects of any kind). Then came the nuclear disaster at Chernobyl in 1983, which resulted in 59 direct deaths and as many as 4,000 others caused by radiation-related cancers. In response, governments in many countries, notably the United States and Japan, stiffened their licensing design requirements and reviewed procedures for nuclear plants, drastically driving up their cost to double or triple the original estimates. As a result, many plans for new plants were canceled, and no new plants were launched in those countries. The market value of nuclear plants fell to 50 percent of their costs in many countries.

France, with fewer fossil fuel resources than any other major European nation, was an exception. Having launched an ambitious program to shift from oil-fired electricity generation to nuclear power after the first oil shock, France stuck with its program despite the accidents at Three Mile Island and Chernobyl, and continued to expand its nuclear energy sector. Today, France has 59 nuclear reactors (second only to the United States) that provide between 75 and 80 percent of the nation's electricity needs, and its consumer electricity rates are among the lowest in the EU.

The second building cycle in electricity capacity was the move to natural gas starting in the 1990s. Seeing an opportunity to capitalize on sustained low natural gas prices and the emergence of highly efficient natural gas combined cycle (NGCC) generating technology, investors built smaller, cleaner, less expensive, and more easily constructed NGCC plants. Then gas prices ran up, leaving a glut of underutilized gas-generating capacity. The market value of natural gas plants assets fell, on average, by 40 percent.

In both of these capacity-building episodes, the power industry's decision to invest heavily in a new technology turned out badly. In the nuclear case, consumers bore much of the cost, whereas in the case of gas, deregulation shifted much of the risk (and the cost) from the consumer to the owners of the generation assets. There were a number of bankruptcies, and the surviving power companies spent the early years of this decade repairing their balance sheets and reducing their risk profiles. They remain very wary as they plan for new baseload generation five or ten years from today.

THE PRODUCERS' DILEMMA

Power generators, still heavily dependent on coal, face great uncertainties today as they choose which technologies and fuel sources to invest in, including the future price of natural gas, the future regulation and potential price of greenhouse gas emissions, and the true cost of alternatives for building new generation capacity, including nuclear energy and renewables such as wind and solar energy.

If greenhouse gas emissions are restricted in the United States, as they already are in Europe, for example, the burden of adjustment is likely to fall on the nation's existing fleet of coal-fired power plants. Other sectors of the economy would continue expanding their emissions as they grow, albeit at a slower rate as a result of corporate average fuel efficiency (CAFE) limits and other potential efficiency gains in transportation, while the coal-fired fleet brings down its emissions far enough and fast enough to offset their expansion and still meet the economywide reduction targets.

The reason is economic. In most sectors, reducing the emissions from a stationary source requires separating out the greenhouse gases from the flue-gas stream and sequestering them. The cost of doing this with today's technology generally—which, as we have seen, has not yet been tested at commercial levels—is estimated to be $80 to $100 per ton sequestered. However, the power-generation sector has another alternative available: replacing existing coal-fired plants with newly built plants using an alternative generation technology that has much lower greenhouse gas emissions, such as NGCC (the same solution that led to losses in the 1990s). At current prices, the all-in cost of replacing coal with NGCC amounts to only $30 to $40 per ton of emissions avoided. As a result, regulators have strong incentives to meet their emissions targets by closing down coal-fired plants before significantly restricting other stationary sources.

That could happen fairly rapidly. If U.S. emissions are merely capped at 2006 levels with no actual reductions, then expansion elsewhere in the economy would cause about half of today's coal-fired production to be replaced over the next 20 years. And more aggressive targets would lead to correspondingly faster replacement.

This logic cuts both ways. Most U. S. politicians favor implementing greenhouse gas (GHG) restrictions through some sort of economywide cap-and-trade scheme that puts a market price on GHG emission allowances. But at what price? The lowest price that will hold economywide emissions flat (let alone reduce them) must be high enough to motivate companies to favor new plant construction for fuels other than coal. At natural gas prices in the range of $7 to $8 per 1,000 cubic feet (about 1 million Btus) that means emissions allowances trading at $30 to $40 per ton of CO_2 equivalent or more. An allowance price of about $65 or more, however, would be needed to force the replacement of existing coal-fired plants. Since natural gas is the favored alternative, in effect, the price of gas sets the price of emissions allowances over a fairly wide range (see Exhibit 8-3).

This is happening in other jurisdictions. The European Union has imposed a broad-based cap-and-trade program for GHG emissions. The program had a clumsy start, with an unsustainable level of emission allowances issued in the first round; but it has now moved to a second round, with allowances more closely managed. The market has priced these second-round allowances at $30 to $40 per ton, since the cost of converting from coal to natural gas is roughly the same in Europe as it is in the United States.

Power producers will thus be forced to make some bets as they plan for expanding power-generation capacity in

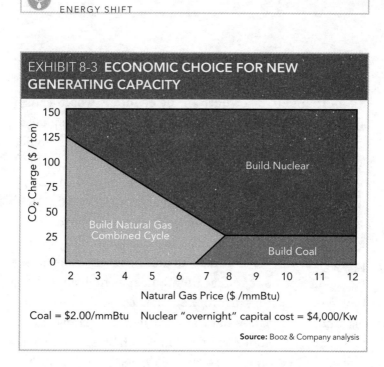

EXHIBIT 8-3 ECONOMIC CHOICE FOR NEW GENERATING CAPACITY

CO$_2$ Charge ($ / ton)

Build Nuclear

Build Natural Gas Combined Cycle

Build Coal

Natural Gas Price ($ /mmBtu)

Coal = $2.00/mmBtu   Nuclear "overnight" capital cost = $4,000/Kw

Source: Booz & Company analysis

the short to intermediate term, and given the capital costs and long-term nature of power generation equipment, these bets will affect their fortunes for decades.

Betting on coal seems highly risky today. As we have noted, the future of coal-fired generation under most commonly discussed carbon regimes appears bleak based on the extremely high cost of separating postcombustion greenhouse gases from a flue-gas stream using today's carbon capture and sequestration (CCS) technology—estimated at $80 to $100 per ton of CO$_2$ equivalent. What are the prospects for CCS costs improving dramatically? Over the long term, quite good; separation and sequestration, according to a Booz & Company analysis, could be available for about $30 per ton by 2020. More broadly, coal-gasification technology could offer a potential pathway for employing coal that avoids the need for expensive postcombustion separation. Unfortunately, traditional gasification technologies with CCS become economic only if natural gas prices rise significantly. However, new gasification technologies may be emerging that could be cost-effective at lower gas prices. Today, these technologies exist only at small scale, but their potential for an extraordinary impact should not be overlooked. Their impact would cut two ways. On the one hand, it would revive the fortunes of coal mining, replacing LNG as the source of incremental gas supplies. On the other hand, it would accelerate the shift away from conventional coal-fired generation.

Natural gas seems like a more reasonable bet for power generation today. But the outlook for gas is dependent on the availability of sufficient supplies at a reasonable price. As noted in Chapter 6, the prospects for natural gas are bright in North America, given expanded estimates of potential reserves that include unconventional gas sources. Other regions, however—notably the EU—will need to import gas to make up for dwindling domestic supplies, mostly in the form of liquefied natural gas, for incremental supply. Thus LNG is likely to set the long-term price for all natural gas. But LNG is a globally traded commodity with a more or less global price, like crude oil, not a collection of separate local/regional markets, like electricity.

Power producers could also bet that the nuclear renaissance will turn out to be real. Nuclear power will look increasingly attractive if greenhouse gas restrictions are enacted. And if the price of natural gas rises, nuclear generation stands as the principal economic alternative to natural gas as a source of low-GHG electricity, putting an effective cap on LNG prices globally. But as noted in the previous chapter, the costs of building nuclear capacity are uncertain, and the variety of safety and security concerns involved make decisions to build new plants as much a political and social as an economic question. Nevertheless, the global nature of the LNG market makes the nuclear alternative effectively available everywhere. If the global price of LNG (and the linked price of GHG emissions) rises too far, then a power company somewhere in the world will shift its next power plant from gas-fired to nuclear, and all power consumers will benefit from the resulting price cap. But given the costs and risks of nuclear, it is likely that strong governmental support would be a precondition for large-scale development of nuclear power generation.

The final bet is on renewable energy sources, especially wind and solar energy. There's no question that these are among the most promising alternatives for supplying the world's future electricity needs in the long term. Renewables, as we have seen, could be making double-digit market-share inroads into electricity generation by 2020 if technological advances and government subsidies continue and industry forecasts prove accurate. They have been commanding tremendous amounts of attention in recent years and are attracting large amounts of investment capital and government subsidies, especially in the United States and Europe. But the commercial risks for power producers are high in the current economic environment, since they remain largely uncompetitive on cost without subsidies. One of the key determinants for renewables is thus likely to be the scope and durability of governmental support.

The uncertainties and questions that surround the puzzle over power generation have been overwhelming during the last few years, leading to the current situation of turmoil and inaction in building new power generation capacity in developed countries. How quickly, and how seriously, will governments pursue greenhouse gas restrictions? Will fossil fuel prices remain high enough in the future to keep nuclear and renewable energy competitive with other fuels? How big a factor will the expanded supply of unconventional gas become? Can "clean coal" technology with carbon capture and storage be developed and deployed fast enough to fill the capacity gap? How expensive will the new technology ultimately prove to be? How fast will technological breakthroughs happen in solar power? For many in the power-generation industry, the answer to these uncertainties— and one of the safer bets for many companies—may be to pursue a broad portfolio of energy sources. (See "Where Politics Meets Arithmetic.")

WHERE POLITICS MEETS ARITHMETIC by David Gee

As we confront the problem of ensuring adequate energy supplies in a carbon-constrained future, everyone is looking for a silver bullet—some magic technology that's going to solve the world's energy problems. But there is no silver bullet. In fact, there are challenges, at least in the short term, with all the potential solutions.

For example, one of the misconceptions today is that we will easily be able to meet all future demand with renewables and hence make the need for fossil fuel plants obsolete. Renewables are a lot harder to execute and more costly than many people think. One problem is that wind and solar energy are intermittent energy sources, meaning that they typically only partially count toward capacity goals for reliability-planning purposes (e.g., sometimes only 10 percent of their nameplate capacity is considered usable for capacity-planning purposes). Another is that there's a lot of wind and sunshine, but they are not always found where the demand for electricity is, so you need to build transmission lines, which makes projects much more expensive and creates more possible opponents. For example, one of the best wind resources in the United States is in South Dakota, but the large markets like Chicago are 1,000 miles away. And even renewable projects run into local opposition (e.g., NIMBYs). The Cape Wind project off Cape Cod is one excellent example. Solar energy is promising, but it isn't economic right now, and it is unclear how quickly the costs of technology will come down. In addition, wind turbine and solar panel production capacity is finite and running at 100 percent. Biomass is also promising, but fuel supply-chain and quality-control problems make its economic radius limited to approximately 50 to 100 miles of a plant site, limiting its potential overall volume.

Another common perception is that demand response can solve all of our problems and has negative costs. There are multiple barriers to fully benefiting from demand response efforts. The most common example is the agency risk of new buildings or homes. The developer wants to lower the up-front cost of a new home or new office space to maximize its marketability, so he has limited incentive to pay the higher costs of more economic and more energy-efficient construction (e.g., triple-glazed windows in new office buildings). While they profess interest in energy efficiency, most buyers are still focused on the up-front costs.

These are all very pragmatic, practical issues. This is where politics meets arithmetic. So, yes, we can add capacity with renewables or demand response programs—and from a policy point of view, we absolutely should do so. It is just going to be harder and more expensive than many people think, and we are not going to be able to build new renewable energy capacity at anything like the volumes that some people are bandying about. While these actions are politically appealing, if one does the arithmetic on how much of an impact renewables or demand response can have in reality in the near to mid-term, they are part of—but not the only—solution. There is just not enough volume to meet the growth in demand. Moreover, almost all of the nonfossil fuel programs will increase the costs of power over and above the levels at which they would otherwise have been. In some cases we are already beginning to see state utility commissions raise questions concerning the costs of these mandates, another form of arithmetic meeting politics.

Coal is the most economic solution for power generation, but it has become the bête noire of the industry because of uncertainty about the costs of capture and sequestration technologies for CO_2 emissions. There's very little interest in building coal plants from our U.S. clients right now. With natural gas, the technology is straightforward, but there is significant uncertainty about prices in the future. Nevertheless, gas seems like the most popular approach for new capacity in the short term, which in itself should put more upward pressures on gas prices. With nuclear energy, we are seeing many applications for licenses for new plants in the United States, but the capital commitments are huge and the costs uncertain; the engineering, procurement, and construction (EPC) costs have been breathtakingly high in recent years. Fewer than 10 to 15 new plants are likely to be built in the next several years, and none of them will be operating before 2017. For all kinds of energy projects, the demand for new plants and infrastructure around the world today has been so high that EPC costs have risen sharply. Everything is becoming more capital-intensive.

What we will need to do is to get away from the silver bullet mindset, and instead deal with the more boring and executionally intensive challenge of pursuing a broad portfolio of energy solutions—renewables, demand response, coal, gas, and so on. There is no single technology or energy source that is big enough to be the sole answer.

David Gee is executive vice president of AES Corp. and president of its North America group. AES, based in

Arlington, Virginia, generates power through 121 power plants worldwide from a wide range of fuel sources, including natural gas, coal, oil, petroleum, coke, wind, biomass, and water. The company also operates electric utilities in six countries, and has announced plans to invest as much as $10 billion over the next 5 to 10 years in alternative energy, including wind generation, liquefied natural gas (LNG), and visionary climate-change technologies.

The most likely path for the power generation industry for the developed countries in the near future seems to rule out major coal development and to favor natural gas as the preferred fuel for incremental new capacity. This is certainly the case in North America. There will be some scope for increases in nuclear capacity in the United States, but it will need to be driven by government policy and, possibly, government financing. In Europe and other regions, the trade-offs will be tougher in balancing the imperatives of greenhouse gas restrictions with the geopolitical exposure of using natural gas imports and the risks and costs of nuclear. Across the world, the share of renewables will increase, but barring significant increases in government support it will happen too slowly to have a significant effect on the overall mix of fuels over the next two decades.

But while the problems in solving the power-generation puzzle may be formidable, so are the opportunities. The electric power sector, worldwide, is overdue for a building boom. Governments and investors need to build new capacity to replace older plants, while also building new ones to meet anticipated growth, especially in the developing world. The combined demand for replacement of old plants and the building of new plants means that about two-thirds of the power-generating capacity that will be on line in 2030 has yet to be built—providing enormous scope for effecting change. Meanwhile, investors are spending massively on research, development, and commercialization of new energy technologies. Given the magnitude of the business opportunity that the energy shift of the next decades will provide, significant innovations in future power generation are possible—perhaps even the development of breakthrough technologies that will change the existing rules of the game.

9

CONCLUSION: APPROACHING THE ENERGY SHIFT

AS THE PRECEDING chapters of this book have shown, the turmoil in the energy markets today is a sign of sweeping changes in the world's industrial, commercial, and consumer landscapes—changes that will continue for decades to come. Our civilization is discovering that the way we produced and used energy throughout the twentieth century is unsustainable in the twenty-first. The shift to a less petroleum-intensive, less carbon-emitting world that relies heavily on new technologies has begun. But how will it play out over the next 5 to 20 years?

There is no shortage of predictions and forecasts. Some observers are alarmists, warning that we have waited too long to act, and that the world will inevitably experience serious economic and environmental disruptions.

Others are utopians, claiming that we will solve all our problems with some simple "silver bullet" plan. Mainstream forecasters earnestly attempt to predict future prices, supply-and-demand trends, and market shares for various fuels decades hence. All of these predictions are likely to be wrong, and if history is any guide, many of them will be very wrong indeed. Five or ten years ago, many experts foresaw the rise in energy demand among the industrializing Asian nations—but they underestimated the limits on supply response and the run-up in capital costs. So few, if any, imagined that petroleum prices would soar to the more than $100 per barrel level reached in 2008.

To think effectively about the future of energy, you need to simplify—to consider the most critical factors that, depending on their speed and breadth, will shape the energy shift going forward. There are, above all others, three major factors to consider. The first is the future path of global greenhouse gas regulation, the second is the future level of concern about energy security, and the third is the future pace of technological development. Every nation, company, and individual should seek to understand and carefully consider all three of these factors, as the way they unfold will determine the success or failure of the energy-related decisions that we make today.

THE SHIFT SO FAR

The energy shift is already under way, driven by rising demand, constrained supplies, and—most recently—concerns about CO_2 emissions and their link to climate change. The scientific consensus about the dangers of global warming has taken deep root in political and popular opinion, and some energy policies have already been reoriented around low-carbon solutions. Corporations in both the transportation and the power-generation sector have made energy alternatives a critical part of their strategy. "You'd better believe that [climate change] is going to be a major issue," said Enel CEO Fulvio Conti in a recent interview about his own company's strategy, "because it may be too late to resolve the problem later on. And environmental sustainability also happens to be a good business proposition. If you're an energy company, you have to work with this reality. You want to have the most diverse sourcing of your raw materials possible to get to a position where you can effectively combat climate change."

In transportation, the shift away from petroleum has created significant interest and investment in alternative fuels and power trains. A range of technologies is now viable, including biofuel, flex-fuel, and hybrid cars. In addition, plug-in hybrids (and all-electric and hydrogen-powered vehicles) are now technically feasible. Brazil has demonstrated that biofuels can supply transportation needs on a mass scale, although concerns about the land-use and carbon impact of biofuels remain. The hybrid car is the most successful alternative power train so far, and it seems poised to gain significant additional market share in the near future. Consumer interest is intense in many nations, and automakers (many of them caught flat-footed by the events of the past few years) are rushing to put new hybrid models into production. The next iteration of environmentally friendlier automotive power trains, the plug-in hybrid, is very close to mass production, and market conditions seem favorable for its adoption.

In the electricity-generation sector, the prospect of a lower-carbon future has already had significant effects on the coal industry and power producers, leading to the delay or cancellation of hundreds of new coal-fired power plants that had been proposed over the last few years. At the same time, it has caused a surge of interest in building natural gas power plants. It has also given a tremendous boost to alternative energy sources for power generation, brightening the outlook especially for wind and solar power, although they still provide only a small share of world electricity today. Finally, it has led to a reconsideration of nuclear energy. A few years ago, nuclear seemed dead; today, new constuction is under way again, although it is still limited to some countries and regions, and it is still in its early stages.

THE SHIFT GOING FORWARD

But so far, despite the sea change in public opinion, the torrents of media attention, and the worldwide surge of activity in research, development, and planning, there has not been sufficient change in the reality of energy production to significantly shorten the timetable for the energy shift. Low-carbon, renewable energy sources still supply only a small fraction of global energy needs. With energy demand likely to double over the next two decades, the likelihood is that the use of fossil fuels will simply double as well, even as the use of low-carbon fuels expands. And world greenhouse gas emissions will inexorably increase.

How fast the shift to low-carbon fuels takes place, both in transportation and in power generation (as well as the composition of the world's absolute energy mix in 2030 and beyond) will depend largely on how the three major areas of uncertainty are resolved. In each of these three areas, we see one overarching uncertainty—a challenge waiting to be resolved, with the resolution still unclear. In other words, there are three bifurcations ahead—three decision points with dramatic first-order implications for the companies in the energy industry itself, and large second-order implications for the rest of us.

The first area of uncertainty is the future of greenhouse gas regulation. Popular and political support for combating climate change has advanced impressively over the past decade. However, thus far few taxpayers and consumers have been called upon to pay the costs. The reduction in emissions that experts think is needed to avoid permanent climate-related damage to human civilization and global ecology will be costly. It remains to be seen whether the impetus for change will strengthen if the prices of transportation fuels, electricity, and energy-intensive goods rise high enough to make the costs of innovation seem low by comparison. And if the costs of fuel level off or diminish, it's not yet clear whether government regulation, based on concerns about climate change, will force the necessary innovations anyway.

Furthermore, the planetwide nature of climate change means that regional or national regulation will tend to be ineffective unless a global agreement can be reached. Negotiating such an agreement may prove to be one of the most difficult exercises in the history of international diplomacy. The main stumbling block for global climate change policy in the developed world to date—the opposition of the United States—seems likely to fade. Public attention is thus likely to focus on changes in U.S. policy and the negotiations leading up the next round of global talks to enact a successor to the Kyoto treaty, scheduled for late 2009 in Copenhagen.

The most important single development to watch for— the crux of this bifurcation—is whether the leading industrialized nations, perhaps under the auspices of the G8 (Canada, France, Germany, Italy, Japan, Russia, the United Kingdom, and the United States), prove both willing and able to reach an agreement with the major industrializing nations, particularly China and India, to significantly reduce CO_2 emissions. The latter are likely to insist on wealth and technology transfers to help them install clean coal technology in new plants and replace dirty coal plants with either clean coal, nuclear, gas, or renewable energy technologies. The costs would be considerable, and selling this idea to taxpayers in developing nations may prove challenging.

If the uncertainty of greenhouse gas regulation is resolved by the enactment of a global framework that includes both developed and industrializing nations, higher costs will be mandated for CO_2 emissions, and thus for all users of fossil fuels. The impact will be dramatic and immediate for several very large sectors of the world economy, including energy producers, electric utilities, and transportation companies.

In a world with high mandated costs for CO_2 emissions, the competitive advantage of companies whose fortunes are based on fossil fuels would suffer—including, broadly speaking, all the incumbent companies in the coal and oil and gas industries. On the other hand, opportunities would open for the entire range of companies pursuing low-carbon alternatives. Nuclear and renewable energy would receive the boost they need if they are to spread at a much faster pace. Energy companies that invested in these technologies early would have a head start over their competitors, and might well be favored for expansion. Corporate leaders in these industries, of course, are keenly aware of this, and are studying the implications closely and devising strategies for survival in whatever environment prevails. (See "Ready for a Scramble; Hoping for a Blueprint."). Some of them, inevitably, will feel forced to bet heavily on nonfossil fuel innovation. Given the start-up costs, these bets will turn the companies into global industry leaders if they succeed and will be devastating for the companies if they fail.

READY FOR A SCRAMBLE; HOPING FOR A BLUEPRINT by Graeme Sweeney

Society faces critical choices about how it wants the global energy system to develop over the next 50 years. We're seeing a step change in the rate of growth of energy demand. The supply of conventional oil and natural gas that is relatively easy to extract won't be able to keep up. This is not to say that oil is suddenly going to run out, but just as energy demand is surging, many of the world's conventional oil fields are going into decline. In fact, all the world's energy sources—hydrocarbons, renewables, and alternatives together—will struggle to match demand. Society will have to reach new levels of energy efficiency, and we are going to need all the energy we can get. At the same time, environmental strains—both climate change and local pollution—are increasing and are placing constraints on the manner in which energy producers can act.

If you look at possible scenarios for the future, two routes seem possible. One is a "scramble" scenario, in which companies and nations rush to secure energy resources, fearing that energy security is a zero-sum game in which some will win while others lose. In this scenario, the use of local coal and home-grown biofuels increases very quickly, taking the path of least of resistance, and policy makers are quite likely to pay little attention to actually curbing energy consumption until supplies actually run short. Likewise, despite a lot of conversation, greenhouse gas emissions are not seriously addressed until major shocks trigger severe political reactions, leading to energy price spikes and volatility. The result is a turbulent and uncomfortable world.

The second route is a "blueprint" scenario, in which the challenges of energy security, energy supply, and the environment are anticipated, and coalitions of the willing emerge in the private sector and at the local and national governmental levels to take the lead. Much innovation occurs. At the local level, major cities develop links with industry to reduce local emissions. National governments introduce efficiency standards, taxes, and other policy instruments; harmonization increases; and policies converge across the globe. We establish a substantial capability for carbon dioxide capture and storage. The result is a more stable energy system and a much better environmental outcome.

Royal Dutch Shell plc has a strategy to ensure that we have a successful business in either scenario, but we have a clear preference for living and working in a world in which the blueprint approach leads to a more stable energy system and a more stable environment. This future offers a better pathway not only to provide enough energy for economic growth, but also to manage greenhouse gas emissions. We believe that Shell has a role to play by increasing the efficiency of our operations, establishing a substantial capability to capture carbon dioxide and store it safely, continuing to research and develop technologies that increase efficiency and reduce emissions, leading the sustainable development of biofuels and other low-CO_2 sources of energy, and promoting the responsible use of energy. We are committed to working with society and governments to move toward that better future. It will happen only if policy makers can agree on an overall set of approaches and actively promote energy efficiency and new technology for important sectors of the economy, including heat and power generation, industry, transport, and buildings. Time is short. We have to move with the same urgency, ingenuity, and persistence that put humans on the moon and created the digital age.

Graeme Sweeney is executive vice president of future fuels and CO_2 at Royal Dutch/Shell Group. He has held numerous positions previously with the company, including president of Shell Global Solutions in the United States and vice president, manufacturing supply and distribution for Shell Europe Oil Products. Dr. Sweeney has recently been elected as chairman of the Advisory Council of the European Technology Platform of Zero Emission Fossil Fuels Power Plants (ETP-ZEP). He is also a member of the Gleneagles Dialogue Project Steering Board and the UK Energy Research Partnership.

The second-order effects will also have widespread impacts across all industries. Many managers are just beginning to realize how their companies might be affected. Energy-intensive industries such as steelmaking and aluminum smelting would see their cost structures rise. But any company that deals with goods that are shipped over long distances would also be affected by higher transportation costs. This could affect long-term decisions about offshoring, for example. Some manufacturing will be sourced closer to retail markets, and the future will favor some dramatic changes in logistics: for example, more flexible supply-chain footprints, in which the flow of goods can be reconfigured rapidly as fuel and transportation options change. Energy efficiency measures would also be favored in this future, although the "low-hanging fruit" of easy savings has already been realized in many parts of industry.

If the uncertainty over greenhouse gas regulation is resolved by a *failure* to achieve a worldwide accord, however, the energy shift will proceed far more slowly, leading to very different impacts on industry. The momentum for slowing the growth of CO_2 emissions would be likely to dissipate. Individual nations would have less of an incentive to agree to limits and might put their national interests in energy security and economic development first, leading to backsliding. There is some evidence that this is already happening. In several developed nations, including Italy and the United States, applications to build new coal-fired power plants were approved in recent years, and many new coal plants are being built in developing nations like China and India. In addition, national governments would be less likely to continue subsidies for solar and wind power (many such subsidies are short-term) or to increase incentives and regulatory support for building nuclear capacity. The overall shift to lower-carbon energy sources would take far longer, and the current uncertainty about the future of energy would continue, with the current incentives remaining in place.

Even if the pace of regulation is slower, some measures, like the flexible supply-chain footprint, will still be worthwhile. The urgency will be diminished, however, and it will take longer to realize the investments made in them. A few winning companies may build their long-term reputations on being early adopters of low-carbon logistics, but 20 years or more may pass before they feel the full impact.

The second major area of uncertainty is energy security. Concerns about the political stability of oil supplies have been and will continue to be an important driver of national and regional energy policies. Again, we see a likely bifurcation: either the world energy markets will continue to become more global, with increasing trade in energy resources and energy technologies, or the markets will turn inward toward trade within regions and nations.

In a world in which trade in energy continues to expand, different fuels and technologies will tend to compete globally based on their intrinsic characteristics, including cost, convenience, and environmental impact. This will have particular impact on the use of natural gas, which, because of the development of liquefied natural gas infrastructure, is becoming an increasingly global commodity that is especially suitable for electricity generation (because of its relatively low output of greenhouse gases).

But if energy-security concerns push nations and businesses toward more regional and national solutions, decisions about future energy sources will be driven more by questions of geography and resource availability than by economic or environmental factors. With more than 40 percent of total natural gas reserves concentrated in the Middle East, and 15 percent in Iran (although one recent study estimates that U.S. reserves may be much larger than past estimates suggested), the future of gas as a widely available global commodity could become uncertain. The prospect of a fragmented energy market is still more likely if major gas producers, including Russia and the Middle Eastern nations, form an OPEC-like cartel. (The Iranian government proposed such an arrangement in 2007 and has held discussions with other gas-producing nations.) Energy-consuming nations would look to any sources they could find without political cost. And this would increase the pressure to develop clean coal technology, and to speed the development of wind, solar, and nuclear energy.

Moreover, increasing concerns about energy security would encourage energy-importing countries to act more purely in their self-interest and to pay less attention to environmental constraints. The United States, for example, would be more likely to develop biofuels on a large scale, to expand coastal and Arctic oil drilling, and to exploit its large reserves of oil sands, oil shale, and coal as a matter of course. Other nations in Asia and Latin America with their own reserves would do the same. Europe might turn to coal imports, large-scale biofuels development, and nuclear energy to reduce its dependence on Russian and Middle Eastern natural gas. This more fragmented global energy industry would have implications for companies with global, integrated supply chains, once again requiring them to build in more flexibility to cope with regional and national differences in energy usage. Some companies might have to choose which regions to operate within, based on their ability to reach cooperative agreements with the governments involved.

The third area of uncertainty is the pace of technological innovation. In many spheres of energy production and consumption, research and development that could significantly change the underlying rules of the energy game is under way today. As we have noted throughout this book, technological development is difficult to predict, particularly in energy, because the *invention* of new technologies is not enough. A new technology requires a new infrastructure. But we are at the stage in history where seemingly small technological changes could trigger major systemwide innovations in a 10- or 20-year time frame. In power generation, for example, a breakthrough in carbon sequestration and storage technology could lead to a renaissance in coal-fired electricity production, giving an advantage to energy companies with existing coal supply lines and putting increasing cost pressures on the entire range of alternative fuels, from natural gas to renewables. On the other hand, a step-change advance in solar energy efficiency and storage could challenge many of the existing assumptions about electricity generation.

In both these cases, the second-order effects would be vast. Consider railroads—just part of the extensive supply chain that's been built up over the decades to move coal. In a world in which clean coal is favored, railroads become even more important; in a world in which solar power is ascendant, one of railroads' chief activities would dwindle, and their greatest assets might become the rights of way for stringing electric power transmission lines where trains used to carry coal.

The impact of technological breakthroughs could be similarly consequential for automobile manufacturers and their suppliers. If technological advances in alternative power trains are slow to develop, the internal combustion engine could remain competitive for decades to come. Biofuels might become an increasingly attractive alternative, leading to major changes in land use and infrastructure. But what if innovations in alternative power trains come quickly? The computer industry is famous for Moore's Law: the observation, first made by Intel engineer Gordon Moore, that computer power per dollar was doubling about every 18 months, and would continue to do so. Moore's Law has held true for four decades, and it has been an enormous driving force for global prosperity and quality of life (and has bolstered the wealth of a great many companies and individuals). Less well known is the presence of a Moore's Law equivalent in battery technology: the efficiency of batteries has been improving steadily at a rate of about 7 percent per year for the last two decades. This means that it doubles about every eight years, not nearly as fast as computer power but fast enough to dramatically accelerate the energy shift in transportation by 2030—at least if it continues or improves. (And billions of dollars in R&D are being spent to speed this trend.) Once batteries become cheap and efficient enough to make all-electric cars more practical and cost-effective, we could see the obsolescence of the entire infrastructure that has been set up to manufacture, refine, transport, and sell petroleum products. Biofuels might be bypassed, and at the same time, a huge new source of energy demand would open for electric utilities.

One important indicator for tracking the potential impact of technology is to watch where governments place their bets, and how big those bets are. In power generation, government policy has driven the notable shifts among power-generation fuels in the past. For example, in France, a lack of fossil fuel resources led to the creation of the country's nuclear capacity, which provides a larger share of electricity today than in any other nation. Another example is Denmark, where the drive for energy independence after the oil crises of the 1970s gave birth to its market-leading wind energy industry. In transportation as well, past shifts in fuel usage have largely been the result of government policy. Brazil's decision to create an ethanol industry and infrastructure in the 1970s, for example, set the stage for the large-scale adoption of flex-fuel vehicles; Europe's collective decision to provide tax advantages for diesel over gasoline created the conditions for the shift to diesel power trains over the past decade.

STRATEGIES TO SPEED THE SHIFT

So what happens when you combine an accelerating social force (greenhouse gas regulation), a vacillating political scene (energy security), and burgeoning potential discontinuity (technological change)? The short answer is that no one knows. There are no obvious parallels in history.

But it is possible to suggest some strategies nonetheless, at both the macro (national and international) and the micro (company-focused) levels.

Looking back at the history of energy, we know that major shifts have often taken many decades to occur. The first commercially viable steamship, for example, was launched in 1807, yet it was not until the 1850s that steamships became competitive with sailing ships in terms of speed, and steam did not entirely supplant sail power for several more decades. In the early days of electricity, alternating current (the kind that powers the world today) was developed in the 1880s, and the first commercial power plant began operating in California in 1893. The new technology enabled the long-distance distribution of electric power, but in some regions of the United States, electricity became widely available only in the 1950s. Nuclear energy was first deployed as a source of electric power more than half a century ago, in the 1950s, but its progress stopped in the 1970s as a result of concerns about safety—even though, as the industry's subsequent safety record shows, those concerns were overblown.

Today, given the future demands for increased energy and the constraints imposed by climate change, the world can't afford to wait that long for the shift to the low-carbon future. The consequences of inaction may simply be too severe, and the current trajectory of the energy shift is too slow to produce the kinds of massive changes that are needed. Thus, the predominant task of policy makers, business leaders, and the many other constituencies involved in energy is to find ways to accelerate the process. Three strategies must be pursued to speed the energy shift—one in each of the areas of uncertainty that we have identified.

The first strategy is to resolve the uncertainties concerning carbon pricing. A global agreement about carbon emissions, one that includes both the world's major developed nations and the major newly industrializing nations, would provide guidance both for policy makers and for industry about the likely future costs of different energy sources and technologies. Without a widely supported global policy on CO_2 emissions, what happens over the next decade is likely to be what happened over the last one: uncertainty about what kinds of future energy sources and infrastructure will be both feasible and profitable, and, as a result, delays and suboptimal near-term decisions.

But reaching a global carbon agreement will require mechanisms through which the developed world will assist newly industrializing nations in meeting their needs for increasing energy supplies in an environmentally responsible manner. Without such mechanisms, meaningful reductions in world CO_2 emissions are unlikely.

*The second strategy is to elevate the concept of energy secu-
rity from the level of national self-interest to a global level that
reflects the increasing internationalization and interdepend-
ence of energy policies.* So long as nations place short-term
self-sufficiency above long-term energy resilience, concerns about energy security will act as a decelerating force
in the shift to low-carbon fuels. In other words, many nations will be tempted to seek a competitive advantage by
exploiting domestic resources, even if these produce negative environmental outcomes or represent a lost opportunity to prosper from energy innovation. To the extent
that governments view energy security as a long-term
global concern, however, and to the extent that they view
greenhouse gas emissions as a factor that could complicate
their long-term security positions, energy security could
become a force that *accelerates* the energy shift.

Ultimately, nations that place their long-term energy
bets on low-carbon and renewable fuels will increase their
energy security far more than those that take the expedi-
ent route of making short-term bets on secure fossil fuels.
Recent energy history in nations such as Brazil, Denmark,
and France—where policy initiatives of decades past has
led to enhanced energy independence today—supports
this view.

*The third strategy for speeding the energy shift is for govern-
ment and industry to concentrate their bets on future technology in the areas that hold the greatest promise for delivering the
large amounts of low-carbon energy that will be needed in the
coming decades to support economic growth.* Ultimately, of
course, the marketplace is the best arbiter of which technologies are the most promising ones, and government's
record of picking technological winners and losers is

imperfect. But the scale of investment that will be needed to make massive shifts in energy use is so great that a large role for government is already assured.

Nuclear power, for example, is the most scalable currently available technology for producing carbon-free electricity, and nuclear capacity will need to expand if the world is to meet future demand at the same time it reduces carbon emissions. The capital expenditures needed to build nuclear power plants, as well as the regulatory obstacles, make nuclear power a fertile ground for public-private partnerships. Other areas where breakthroughs seem possible, and thus where investment should be focused, include solar energy for electricity generation, carbon sequestration and storage for coal, battery technology to enable advanced hybrids and electric cars, and third-generation biofuels that could create liquid fuels without adverse impact on land use and food prices.

If these strategies break down, then the energy shift will still continue. But in that event the process is likely to be one of great tension, unfulfilled expectations, and difficulties. If the future unfolds in a halting and limited fashion, then come 2030, neither the mix of fuels being used in the world nor the level of greenhouse gases being produced is likely to be materially different from what is the case today. At that point, if the warnings of the world scientific community turn out to be correct, the world would be in the uncomfortable position of experiencing the consequences of global warming, with little time left to undertake corrective action.

On the other hand, if there is successful change in the three critical domains—controlling carbon emissions, redefining energy security, and developing productive new technologies—then the speed of the energy shift will accelerate. This future will not come easily. It may require concerted effort; for example, public-private partnerships may need to finally move from "demonstration" projects to large-scale infrastructure development. There is a growing body of experience with infrastructure projects, in particular, that suggests that when government and business leaders work together in a well-designed managerial structure, they can overcome the delays, cost overruns, and other difficulties that beset big projects. As our colleagues Viren Doshi and Daniel Gabaldon suggested in an article on infrastructure in 2007 ("Lights! Water! Motion!"), much depends on reforming long-established practices, on both the government and the business side, for design and approval, oversight and financing, and construction and operations. For the first time, some leading local governments are experimenting with these reforms—and finding that their ability to build new power and transportation systems is improving accordingly.

THE MICRO PICTURE

We have argued in this book that the most critical decisions will either be made by governments or be the result of large macro forces like supply and demand. Why, then, should a corporate decision maker care? Why pay attention to the energy shift at all? For corporate leaders in the energy industry, the answer is obvious: they already see their business is on the line. But what about the manufacturer, service provider, or small business owner trying to make decisions for the next few years (or months)?

To be sure, if you're reading this passage, you already recognize the impact that the price of energy has on your business or operation. It makes a difference whether you pay $2 or $4 per gallon for oil; it matters what you pay per Btu. But there are more sophisticated ways of looking at this issue. The supply of electricity, for example—whether it is fungible and global, or limited and local—will affect the extent to which you can move operations to emerging nations. Many companies have completely overhauled their supply chains in recent years to take advantage of lower costs in distant places. In a world of fragmented energy supply, it may be more difficult to realize those benefits.

Rather than waiting for the energy shift to take place and reacting accordingly, it is worth looking now at the challenges that may affect your industry. For instance, if you are a food retailer or an apparel manufacturer, you already move many goods over long distances. If the costs of doing this continue to increase, will you be forced to raise prices? Or are you prepared to put in place less costly supply-chain operations, with the same speed and confidence with which you originally sourced your goods from around the world? Are you prepared, for example, to move some of your clothing manufacturing operations back to North America or Europe? Or are you prepared to join many other companies in moving your shipping from motor vehicles back to rail, with its less expensive energy footprint? As we noted earlier, the most resilient companies are already designing flexible supply chains and working out the kinds of alliances and acquisitions that will enable them to keep their options open.

This is not the first time we've seen such a shift. Something analogous happened in the 1970s, when oil companies could no longer easily count on getting crude oil from particular sources of supply. Designers of refineries started developing and implementing "cracking" technologies that allowed them to produce automobile fuel and other products from a variety of types of crude oil. It took several years for these investments to be put in place, but once they had been made, the refining industry was quietly transformed into a much more resilient part of the business.

Other industries will have to cope with second-order effects as well. In the computer services industry, companies from Google to Microsoft are investing in energy innovation as a vehicle to allow them to continue to increase their server capacity. In commodity-oriented processing companies, such as mining and aluminum smelting, some companies have suddenly noticed that their futures depend on their capabilities in energy efficiency and continuous improvement. Companies that produce plastics such as polycarbonates are deeply affected; the costs of shipping their products to manufacturing plants in China, for example, have increased rapidly. Producers of rubber, glass, and electronics components are deeply affected as well.

It's already clear that industries that are highly dependent on fuel—airlines, shipping companies, and power-generation companies—will feel increasing pressure to consolidate. For example, in the airline sector, fuel costs have risen from 10 percent of total annual spending to 30 percent. For this sector, the difficulties of the past few years are probably only the beginning; the airlines cannot sustain their current industry structure as the energy shift continues, and the regulations that have discouraged mergers and acquisitions will no longer be able to hold sway. The single factor that will separate the few winners from the many losers will be the quality of their innovation; Southwest Airlines and a few other peers will continue to have an edge, not so much because of their point-to-point business model, but because of their ingrained practices of business model improvement.

The energy shift will also provide new opportunities for many industries. As new prototypes and experiments are developed, the suppliers of new components and tailored services will be needed. A big solar industry will need plastics, glass, and photovoltaic components; a wind industry will need turbines; and both will need the steel, rubber, copper, and construction services that go into building power transmission lines.

Financial services companies are finding opportunities in innovative financing for infrastructure projects, particularly in the developing world. Human resources–oriented service firms may find great opportunities in training people to compensate for the retirement of skilled energy-industry employees, oil and gas companies may increasingly work on building "digital oil fields," and power producers may look toward "smart grids" and other technology-enhanced innovations in energy supply. Even if the energy mix is fragmented for the next 20 years, and even if the global carbon emission and security problems remain unsolved, the opportunities for joining the energy shift will still continue to grow.

As the three areas of energy uncertainty begin to resolve in the coming years, one other historical fact is worth

remembering: when massive change occurs across industries and across business sectors, it's rare for incumbents
to maintain their preeminent positions. There are count-
less examples of erstwhile corporate behemoths that became extinct as the world around them changed, and
precious few examples of giants that maintained their position by reworking their business models (IBM comes to
mind) or building an unassailable ingrained capability
(Toyota). The preeminent energy company of 2050 may be
an unknown start-up today, building an edge in solar technology that proves to be more valuable than the fossil fuel
reserves of the twentieth century's energy leaders; the
leading automobile company may be built around an innovative electric power train that cancels out the internal
combustion expertise of the incumbent automakers.

Leaders of incumbent companies, and their investors
as well, are keenly aware of this challenge. Given the size
and magnitude of this revolution, and the impact it will
have on every aspect of business, from supply chains to
financing, how many of today's large mainstream companies will be able to survive? It's noteworthy that, of the major companies involved in electricity production in the late
nineteenth century, only one (General Electric) still exists. And as the *Financial Times* noted in 2007, the established oil incumbents of Europe and the United States are
now being eclipsed by a set of new competitors, often with
state ownership, that have built their fortunes on the control of supply at the ground: Saudi Aramco, Gazprom (based
in Russia), China National Petroleum Corporation (CNPC),
the National Iranian Oil Company (NIOC), Petróleos de
Venezuela (PDVSA), Petrobras (in Brazil), and Petronas
(in Malaysia). No incumbent energy or transportation com-

pany, not even these new energy enterprises, can afford to be complacent over the next 20 years. And it is clear that skill in producing old forms of energy and transportation (such as coal-based fuel or internal combustion power trains) may not necessarily translate into skill in producing new forms (such as nuclear or wind energy or electric-based power trains). The incumbents may not have a natural advantage, and they may be held back by their existing customers, employees, and suppliers. In energy in particular, with so many people using established forms of transportation and power, there will be enormous resistance to any significant change, no matter how worthy. It will take truly farsighted, well-managed, and innovative incumbent companies to overcome that resistance.

In short, the speed of the shift is uncertain, the challenges are daunting, and the opportunities couldn't be greater. By 2030, the mix of world fuels can be sharply different, the trajectory of global warming can be improved, and instead of a crisis to be confronted, the world can have proven processes in place to meet the continuing challenges inherent in rising demand, greenhouse gas emissions, and problematic energy supplies. Hopefully, we will all be able to look back and realize that because we helped to accelerate the energy shift in the first years of the twenty-first century, we created the kind of future in which our children and grandchildren around the globe can prosper in a lower carbon, environmentally conscious world.

NOTES

Chapter 2

19 Exhibit 1-1: CAGR = compound annual growth rate.
31 Exhibit 2-2: CAGR = compound annual growth rate. OCED = Organisation for Economic Co-operation and Development.

Chapter 3

43 "In 2005, OPEC accounted for 42 percent of world oil production; by 2030, as non-OPEC reserve growth slows . . .": *Key World Energy Statistics 2007*, International Energy Agency.
54 "The Rand Corporation has estimated . . .": *Oil Shale Development in the United States: Prospects and Policy Issues*, The Rand Corporation (2005).

Chapter 4

69 "Indeed, studies such as the International Energy Agency's 2004 *Biofuels for Transport* report . . .": *Biofuels for Transport: And International Perspective*, International Energy Agency (2004).
70 "And studies recently published in *Science* found that when this initial carbon dioxide deposit is taken into account . . .": "Use of U.S. Croplands for Biofuels Increases Greenhouse Gases Through Emissions from Land-Use Change," *Science*, February 2008.

Chapter 5

85 "Currently, coal ranks second to oil as a producer of CO_2 emissions . . .": *International Energy Outlook 2007*, Energy Information Administration, U.S. Department of Energy.

94 "A recent study by the Massachusetts Institute of Technology . . .": *The Future of Coal: Options for a Carbon-Constrained World*, Massachusetts Institute of Technology (2007).

Chapter 6

110 "The International Energy Agency (IEA) expects LNG shipments to grow 6.6 percent . . .": *World Energy Outlook 2007*, International Energy Agency.

Chapter 7

131 "Developing 5 percent of the North Sea's surface area, the association says . . .": *Delivering Offshore Wind Power in Europe*, The European Wind Power Association (2008).

131 "In the United States, a recent report by the Department of Energy concluded . . .": *20% Wind Energy By 2020: Increasing Wind Energy's Contribution to U.S. Energy Supply*, Office of Scientific and Technical Information, U.S. Department of Energy (2008).

139 "The EU found that half its member countries need to provide . . .": *The Support of Energy from Renewable Energy Sources*, Commission of the European Communities (2005).

Chapter 8

146 "As Exhibit 8-2 shows, the baseline projections of the International Energy Agency . . .": *World Energy Outlook 2006*, International Energy Agency.

INDEX

ABOUT THE AUTHORS

ERIC SPIEGEL (eric.spiegel@booz.com) is a senior partner at Booz & Company based in McLean, VA, who leads Booz & Company's work for global energy, chemicals, and utilities clients. He has over 25 years of energy and utility consulting industry experience leading major energy client assignments in Asia, the Middle East, Europe, and North and South America. Mr. Spiegel also led Booz & Company's international consulting business in Asia-Australasia-Middle East and lived in Tokyo from 1999 to 2003. His areas of expertise include corporate strategy, mergers and acquisitions, holding company and business unit organization, major capital projects, and major cost restructuring, as well as outsourcing and offshoring, post-merger integration, and procurement and supply chain redesign. Eric holds an MBA from The Amos Tuck Graduate School of Business Administration at Dartmouth College, where he was an Edward Tuck Scholar, and a BA with Honors in Economics from Harvard University. He is a long-standing contributor to *strategy+business* and other publications. Prior to joining Booz & Company, Mr. Spiegel worked with Brown Boveri (now ABB) in marketing and with Temple, Barker & Sloane (now Oliver Wyman) in their energy consulting practice.

NEIL McARTHUR (neil.mcarthur@booz.com) is an Amsterdam-based senior partner at Booz & Company who leads the firm's European business. Mr. McArthur has more than 24 years of experience in the energy, chemicals, and utility industries. He has extensive consulting experience leading major assignments across the globe. His areas of expertise include corporate strategy, and mergers and acquisitions, holding company and business unit organization, postmerger integration, major capital projects and cost restructuring, process redesign and transformation, procurement and supply chain redesign, and shared services design. Neil holds an MBA with distinction from INSEAD and a BSc. (1st class Honors, George Harvey Prize) in civil engineering from the University of Glasgow. He is a Chartered Engineer M.I.Mech.Eng. and a Sainsbury Management Fellow. He has contributed to numerous publications, including the book *CEO: Chief European Officer— Business Leadership in Europe*. Prior to joining Booz & Company, Mr. McArthur worked for Shell International Petroleum B.V. Exploration & Production on assignment in Qatar and the Netherlands.

ROB NORTON (rob.norton@booz.com) is the executive editor of *strategy+business* in New York. He is a former executive editor of *Fortune* magazine, and an adjunct professor at the Graduate School of Journalism at Columbia University. His work has appeared in numerous publications. Rob is editor of *CFO Thought Leaders: Advancing the Frontiers of Finance* and coauthor of *Content Critical: Gaining Competitive Advantage through High Quality Web Content*, and *The Web Content Style Guide: An Essential Reference for Online Writers, Editors and Managers*.

ACKNOWLEDGMENTS

The "future of business" series has been a collaborative effort from the beginning. Our editor and publisher at McGraw-Hill, Herb Schaffner, has been a wise and enthusiastic guide every step of the way—the model of a business book publisher-editor. We have also benefitted from the talents of production manager Ruth Mannino and the rest of the team at McGraw-Hill.

The book was developed and edited under the auspices of *strategy+business*, the quarterly magazine published by our firm. We would like to thank the entire s+b team and, in particular, publisher Jonathan Gage, who helped conceive the project and moved it along at every stage; literary agent Jim Levine, who helped make the book possible; and publicist Mark Fortier and marketing manager Alan Shapiro, who have helped make the book visible. Art Kleiner, editor-in-chief of *strategy+business*, provided editorial oversight and clarity, was involved in the project from conception to final edit, and contributed many of the ideas and approaches that made the book work.

This book would not have been possible without the contributions of many outstanding individuals who make up the talented team at Booz & Company. In particular, we would like to acknowledge the role of Bertram Shelton—

senior adviser to Booz & Company and a former partner who has advised leading petroleum, financial-services, aerospace, and consumer goods worldwide. Without Bert's drive to understand first principles, his passion for ideas, and his ability to find simplicity on the other side of complexity, this book would not be possible. Bert not only gave selflessly of his time but continually challenged the authors and editors to completely think through the issues and to craft a logical but simple story to explain the energy shift. We also owe him a debt of gratitude as an invaluable partner, mentor, and friend throughout our careers.

Our colleagues at the firm have given us the encouragement and support we needed to bring excellence to this project. As part of the "intellectual capital engine," this book benefited from a platform of support and collaborative thought that is rare in any enterprise. Adrienne Crowther, Director of Knowledge Management, played a vital role in coordinating every aspect of this project, as well providing key insights on the book's content. We benefitted greatly from the insights of our current and former colleagues at Booz & Company and at Booz Allen Hamilton who contributed their thoughts, including David Aldrich, Andrew Clyde, Timothy Donohue, Viren Doshi, Molly Finn, Ibrahim El-Husseini, Thomas Flaherty, Juan Carlos Gay, Daniel Gabaldon, Richard Goffi, William Jackson, Cynthia Kibble, Gary Leatherman, George List, Julia Mac-Donald, Joe Martha, Alonzo Martinez, Mark Moran, Nick Pennell, Paolo Pigorini, Harry Quarls, Gary Rahl, Joachim Rotering, Joe Saddi, Ken Saenz, David Sulek, Andrew Steinhubl, Lord Andrew Turnbull, Joseph Vandenberg, Mathijn Wagenmakers, Otto Waterlander, Walter Wintersteller, and James Woolsey.

We also owe a debt of gratitude to the many clients in the energy industry whose experience and insights helped inform the perspective of *Energy Shift*. In particular, we would like to thank those who contributed directly: Murray Smith (the Province of Alberta), Larry Burns (General Motors), Michael J. Quillen (Alpha Natural Resources), T.J. Glauthier (TJG Energy Associates), Joan MacNaughton (ALSTOM Power Systems),Ditlev Engel (Vestas), David Gee (AES), and Graeme Sweeney (Royal Dutch/Shell).